D1536286

iCloud

TOM NEGRINO

 Peachpit Press

Visual QuickStart Guide
iCloud
Tom Negrino

Peachpit Press
1249 Eighth Street
Berkeley, CA 94710
510/524-2178
510/524-2221 (fax)

Find us on the Web at www.peachpit.com
To report errors, please send a note to errata@peachpit.com
Peachpit Press is a division of Pearson Education

Editor: Clifford Colby
Production Editor: Katerina Malone
Compositors: Danielle Foster and David Van Ness
Indexer: Rebecca Plunkett
Cover Design: RHDG / Riezebos Holzbaur Design Group, Peachpit Press
Interior Design: Peachpit Press
Logo Design: MINE™ www.minesf.com

ISBN-13:   978-0-321-81410-4
ISBN-10:   0-321-81410-X

9 8 7 6 5 4 3 2 1

Printed and bound in the United States of America

Dedication

To my wife, Dori, for her support and understanding of a husband who has his cranky days. Here's to fewer of those in the future.

Special Thanks to:

My patient editor, Cliff Colby, who instigated and shepherded this project to completion, made my work better, and encouraged me when a very challenging schedule seemed overwhelming.

Thanks to Katerina Malone, for her excellent production work.

Thanks to the book's compositors, Danielle Foster and David Van Ness, and thanks to Rebecca Plunkett for the index.

Thanks to Peachpit's Nancy Ruenzel and Nancy Davis for their support.

My appreciation to my friends and colleagues at *Macworld* magazine for doing all that testing of iCloud features and writing about it. I'd especially like to single out Jason Snell, Serenity Caldwell, Dan Frakes, Lex Friedman, and Ted Landau for their excellent articles. Mistakes in this book are, of course, entirely my own.

Thanks to Nenad Rondovic (AKA burekbrigada on Elance) for creating a Microsoft Word macro that allowed me to complete this project faster.

Table of Contents

Getting Started with iCloud

Welcome to *iCloud: Visual QuickStart Guide*. This book will help you get up and running with Apple's iCloud online service, which allows your iOS devices (the iPhone, iPad, iPod touch, and Apple TV), your Macs, and your Windows PC to work together in ways that couldn't be done before.

The iCloud service doesn't do just one thing; it's a collection of tools that allows you to better manage your mobile devices, automatically synchronizing your personal information, including calendars, contacts, photos, music, and documents with all your devices. You can use iCloud to find the location of friends, family, and your devices, should those devices (or people) go missing. And iCloud also has added small benefits, such as freeing you from the tyranny of your wireless carrier's over-priced text messaging plans.

In this book, I'll show you how to get the most out of iCloud's various services, allowing you to use your computers and devices and more efficiently. Let's get started.

What Is iCloud?

iCloud is Apple's online service that is, more than anything else, devoted to automatically and seamlessly synchronizing your personal data between all of the devices you may happen to use. First, let me clarify one bit of terminology I'm using in this book. When I refer to a "device," it could be a Mac desktop computer, a Mac notebook computer, or any iOS device, such as an iPhone, iPad, iPod touch, or even the Apple TV. It could even be a Windows PC.

Things have changed quite a bit from the world in which we were tied to our desktop, or even laptop computers. With the advent of the iPhone and the iPad, you might want to check your mail, add to your calendar, edit a contact, or snap a photo when you're away from your computer, and if you have more than one computer, or more than one mobile device, it would be nice if changes you made on one device automatically appeared on all your other devices.

Essentially, that's what iCloud is all about. It liberates you from needing to worry about where your data is. There is no wondering about "Did I take my iPhone photos off the phone and put it on my computer?" or "Did I remember to take that appointment I entered on my iPad and put it on my iMac?" With iCloud, these things simply happen, in the background, and you never have to worry about them. Ideally, all your important data and documents are pushed to all your devices. It's a way to make sure that not just your digital life but your entire life is with you wherever you happen to be.

But really, I tend to think of iCloud as "plumbing in the sky." It doesn't so much do things itself as it enables devices and software to interact with one another in ways that make your life easier.

If, like me, you've been using the Mac for a long time, and you used previous Apple online services such as .Mac and MobileMe, you might be tempted to think that iCloud is just the newest flavor of those services. However, I think that's the wrong way to think about it. Those older services weren't built from the ground up, as iCloud has been, with the idea that your personal information and the documents you create should be ubiquitous and available no matter what device you have within reach.

So let's take the 10,000 foot view of what iCloud can do for you, and I think you'll see that in most cases, it does things that make excellent sense for most of us.

- **Wherever you go, your stuff is there.** In the early days of Mac OS X, there was a program called iSync that allowed you to manually synchronize information (mostly contacts) between mobile phones and a Mac, connected by a wire (or sometimes via Bluetooth). Compared to iCloud, you can think of iSync as roughly equivalent to a stone ax. With iCloud, you can wirelessly synchronize contacts, calendars, email, browser bookmarks, photos, music, apps, documents, and more. You don't have to "initiate a synchronization," and you don't have to do any manual copying, either. All you need do is make or edit something, and it automatically appears on the rest of your devices within a minute or so. So you can shoot a picture on your iPhone, get a decently large-sized view of it on your iPad, then move immediately to your Mac and touch up the photo.

- **You don't need to carry all your stuff with you.** The last time I bought an iPhone, I bought the model with 16 GB of storage. Why that instead of the fat 32 GB model? Because I didn't want to spend the extra $100 to double the storage. I knew that most of the storage space used on an iOS device is taken up by music and video, and I knew that my iTunes library was already far larger than any device I could buy, so I knew that I would always be carrying a subset around with me. Little did I know that Apple was already working on ways to make all of my data available to me, whether I chose to put it on my device or not. With a decent Wi-Fi connection and an optional service called iTunes Match, you can stream the contents of your iTunes library to your iOS device, whether or not you have purchased that content from Apple. You'll find more about using iTunes with iCloud in Chapter 6.

- **Your information is safer, even if you forget**. One of the best things you can do with iCloud is have it automatically backup your iOS devices to Apple's servers, once a day, as long as you have a Wi-Fi connection. That means that if your device is tragically either

lost or stolen, you'll be able to purchase a replacement device, run through the setup process, and restore from the latest backup, without a lot of manual torment. You simply run through the restore process, and your device is in the same state it was the last time iCloud backed it up for you. And from any other iOS device or from the iCloud website, you can remotely lock or erase the data on your wayward device. Don't get me wrong; losing a device is still a pain. But with iCloud, at least it's a pain in your wallet, rather than the pain of identity theft. You'll find more about backing up with iCloud in Chapter 7, and more about remotely locking and erasing an iOS device in Chapter 10.

- **There's less need for wires.** Because iCloud can synchronize many kinds of data and backup your device over a Wi-Fi connection, most of the time you'll only need a USB-to-Dock connector cable to charge your iOS device. Even upgrading to a new version of iOS (once you're on iOS 5) can be done wirelessly; one of the nice little features in iOS 5 are "delta updates," which upgrades only the portion of the operating system that needs it, rather than requiring the whole thing to be downloaded. But in a big conceptual shift, Apple has cut the cord when it comes to iOS devices, meaning that you no longer need a Mac or PC to set them up or maintain them. With iOS 5, the days of needing to plug your iOS device into a computer running iTunes to set it up are gone; a Setup process runs right on the device.

Whether you use the bare minimum of iCloud's services, or you jump in with both feet, iCloud has the ability to blur the location of your data. And that's a good thing. The important thing to understand is that you, personally, won't be dealing so much with iCloud as you will be dealing with the apps on your devices (or, if you prefer, with the iCloud website).

Let's talk a little more about the specific features that iCloud enables. Many of these are familiar, either as apps on your devices, or from use with MobileMe. These features include:

- **Email**. An iCloud account comes with a **me.com** account (if you previously had a **mac.com** account, that will work too; in fact, they are treated as the same account), and email from that account appears on all your devices. iCloud also deals with notes and text messages. You'll find more information about all of these functions in Chapter 2.

- **Contacts and Calendars**. Your address book and calendar information can be shared not only with your own devices but also with other people for whom you give permission. I cover these features in Chapters 3 and 4.

- **Browser Bookmarks**. If you like, you can synchronize your Safari (or on Windows, your Internet Explorer) browser bookmarks via iCloud. You'll find more information about that in Chapter 8.

- **Photos**. Part of iCloud is a new concept called Photo Stream, which pushes the contents of your iOS device's Camera Roll up to the cloud and down to your other devices. Look for more about that in Chapter 5.

- **Synchronized Documents**. In iCloud, you can share documents created in other applications, for example Apple's iWork applications: Keynote, Pages, and Numbers. Documents that you create or edit on one device can update automatically on all your other devices, so no matter what device you're working on, you're always up-to-date. Apple calls this feature Documents in the Cloud, and it's not limited to just Apple's own programs; third-party programs can take advantage of the feature as well. You'll find more information about that in Chapter 9.

- **Location Services**. Using iCloud, you can find the location of people and devices. Again, turn to Chapter 10 for more information on finding and working with people and devices.

All of these services are tied together using storage on Apple's servers. With every iCloud account, you get 5 GB of storage for free, and you can purchase more storage on a yearly basis if needed (up to 50 GB). Some items, such as anything you buy from the iTunes Store and photos in your Photo Stream, don't count against the 5 GB storage quota.

MobileMe Services Missing in iCloud

Apple provided a variety of features in their online services as it evolved, from .Mac to MobileMe and now to iCloud. Some of the original .Mac features were already long gone (anyone remember the iCards online greeting cards? Ironically, they've been resurrected as Cards, a free iPhone or iPod touch app from Apple that lets you shoot pictures on your device and add a note, and Apple prints and mails a physical card for you), including a general Backup service that worked with your Mac.

When Apple announced iCloud, it also heralded the end of MobileMe. MobileMe subscribers who don't make the move to iCloud will lose all access to MobileMe services on June 30, 2012.

Besides the end of MobileMe in general, some of its services will also permanently end with its demise. These services include:

- **iDisk** online storage space (partially offset by iCloud's 5 GB of storage, but less flexible, since you can't mount iCloud storage as a network disk, as you could with iDisk).

- **iWeb site publishing**. Users of iWeb, part of Apple's iLife software suite, must find alternate web site hosting (iWeb allows you to use any Web hosting company). iWeb has been suffering from benign neglect (it got hardly any changes in iLife '11), so I won't be surprised to see the program discontinued altogether in the next iteration of iLife.

- **Gallery**. One of the photo sharing destinations in iPhoto has been MobileMe Gallery, which hosts your pictures on the web. iCloud's Photo Stream isn't a substitute, since you can't view items in the Photo Stream in a Web browser. Instead of the MobileMe Gallery, iPhoto allows you to share photos on Flickr, which is actually a better service; Gallery has been languishing in features and interest for several years.

- **Mac OS X system synchronization**. MobileMe allowed you to synchronize keychains (which contain your system and web passwords), Dock items, System Preferences, Mail accounts, Mail Rules, Mail Signatures, Smart Mailboxes, and Dashboard widgets. A good replacement for keychain synchronization (and the one that I've used for years, because it offers many more features than Apple's old solution) is AgileBits' 1Password (**http://agilebits.com**).

- **Third-party software synchronization**. Many programs, such as Microsoft Entourage, Bare Bones' Yojimbo, The Omni Group's OmniFocus, and Panic's Transmit used MobileMe to synchronize their settings or documents, and when you make the change to iCloud, you'll lose those synchronization services, because the iCloud migration turns off all MobileMe sync features. If you use a program that used MobileMe for synchronization across devices (you can tell because the program will be listed in the Sync tab of the MobileMe preference pane), you should check with the software maker for alternatives, if available. For example, OmniFocus allows you to use Omni's own synchronization server, or any WebDAV server (if you want to handle your own sync server). But as of this writing, Panic hasn't released any alternative for Transmit's synced Favorites.

Hardware and Software Requirements

In order to use iCloud, Apple required users to break with past operating systems and start anew with the latest versions of both their desktop (Mac OS X) and mobile (iOS) operating systems. iCloud also works on recent versions of Microsoft Windows, though many iCloud features work best with or require a Mac.

On the Mac, using iCloud requires that you be running Mac OS X 10.7.2 Lion or later .
That means that iCloud on the Mac has the same hardware requirements as Lion. A Mac requires an Intel Core 2 Duo, Core i3, Core i5, Core i7, or Xeon processor. For portable machines, that includes most of the Intel-based MacBooks (excluding only the original 2006 model); MacBook Pro (if introduced after October 2006); and all models of the MacBook Air. For desktop machines, it includes the Mac mini (mid 2007 or later); iMac (after September 2006); and all versions of the Mac Pro. Your computer needs at least 2 GB of memory (as usual with a Mac, you'll get better performance with more memory), and at least 7 GB of available storage space.

On an iOS device, you must be running iOS 5 or later (as I write this, iOS 5.0.1 has been released); iCloud comes free as part of iOS 5. In fact, much of the amazing

Ⓐ On your Mac, you must be running Mac OS X Lion 10.7.2 or later to use iCloud.

Ⓑ You'll need to be using iOS 5 on your mobile devices to use iCloud features.

things that you can do with iCloud are completely dependent on the features in iOS 5. In terms of hardware, most, but not all, iOS devices are compatible with iOS 5. Any iPhone from the iPhone 3GS or later; any iPad; and the iPod touch 3rd generation or later can run iOS 5, and therefore use iCloud. The 2nd generation Apple TV, which is a modified iOS device, can use iCloud's Photo Stream and iTunes Match services, but the original Apple TV cannot.

On a Windows PC, you can install the iCloud control panel on any version of Windows 7, or Windows Vista with Service Pack 2 or later.

On any platform, you can do some interaction with iCloud services with nothing more than a web browser . I'll discuss the interaction on the iCloud website in each of the chapters that relates to that section of the website.

C The iCloud website allows you to access and work with much of your iCloud data.

Apple ID Considerations

Before you can move to iCloud, you'll need one crucial bit of information: your Apple ID and password. The Apple ID is the glue that holds all your iCloud information together. You may already have an Apple ID, because one is required if you've ever bought anything from the iTunes Store or Mac App Store. And Mac OS X users have been prompted to create an Apple ID when they set up their Macs for years.

The Apple ID must be a valid email address, and is usually a me.com address, which Apple will give to you for free. You'll create and sign into your iCloud account using a single Apple ID, which will then be the Apple ID you use for all iCloud services (but there are caveats; see the "Dealing with Multiple Apple IDs" sidebar later in this section).

Under Mac OS X Lion, your Apple ID can serve as an alternate set of credentials to your usual username and password for services such as file sharing, screen sharing, and account recovery. In Lion, the Apple ID is integrated into the Users & Groups preference pane Ⓐ.

Ⓐ In Lion, there is now an entry for Apple ID in the Users & Groups preference pane.

Dealing with Multiple Apple IDs

Over the years, you may have created more than one Apple ID. For example, you may have created and used a particular Apple ID with the iTunes Store (say, the email address you got from your ISP), and you had a MobileMe address. Both of those can count as Apple IDs. If you previously had a .Mac account, you may have both a **me.com** account and a **mac.com** account, which are aliases of one another. And either can be used as an Apple ID.

The obvious solution would be for Apple to offer the ability to consolidate multiple Apple IDs into one. Unfortunately, if you already have multiple Apple IDs, Apple simply isn't offering that ability as of yet. You do have the option of creating, managing, and resetting the password of your Apple ID account by going to **http://appleid.apple.com**. But by not allowing a person to consolidate multiple Apple IDs they may have picked up over the years, Apple is throwing the management burden onto that person; not exactly consistent with Apple's vaunted philosophy of simplicity.

It's worth pointing out that if you have previously been sharing your Apple ID with others (perhaps because you have been sharing your iTunes library using Home Sharing, or to share purchases from the iTunes Store), those people now have access to your account on a Lion-based Mac, either over a local network or remotely via Back to My Mac. Before you upgrade to iCloud, it's a good idea to reflect upon your security requirements, and if necessary, change the password associated with your Apple ID. Along the same lines, now is the time to think about how secure your Apple ID password is. If it is easily guessable, a word that is in a dictionary, a consecutive sequence of numbers or letters, or otherwise weak, I strongly recommend you change it to a stronger password before moving to iCloud. A quick Google search using the phrase "making a good password" will lead you to much good advice.

If multiple people use a single Apple ID (for example, if your entire family has been using your Apple ID for iTunes Store purchases) you can still do so for that purpose, but each person will have to create a separate Apple ID/iCloud account for syncing and backup of their personal devices.

TIP When I wrote this book, rather than blur my Apple ID in the book's many screenshots, I chose to leave it in readable form. But before the book went to print, I changed the password (which was already pretty good) to an even more secure password.

TIP If you click the Change button in the Users & Groups preference pane under Lion, it's possible to associate your user account with more than one Apple ID.

Configuring iCloud on Your iOS Devices

It's easy to set up iCloud on your iOS device. You can either set it up when you set up iOS 5 for the first time, or you can turn it on at any time. In either event, you'll need an Apple ID. If you don't already have an Apple ID, you can create one during the process.

If you previously had a MobileMe account, there are some other important considerations before you turn on iCloud on your iOS devices. Before you continue in this section, you should first read the "Migrating to iCloud from MobileMe" section, later in this chapter.

To set up iCloud on your iOS device:

1. During iOS 5 initial set up, one of the screens that you will see is the Apple ID screen **A**. If you have already gone through the iOS 5 setup process, skip to step 4.

   You'll need to be connected to a Wi-Fi network during the setup process.

A During iOS 5 setup, you'll be prompted to sign in with an existing Apple ID, or create a new one.

B You can sign in to iCloud in the iCloud pane of the iOS Settings app.

C Once you are signed in to iCloud...

D ... you can turn on the specific services you want to use.

2. Tap Sign In with an Apple ID if you already have an Apple ID.

or

If you need an Apple ID, tap Create or Get (depending on the device) a Free Apple ID. You'll be prompted through the sign-up process, where you'll get a **me.com** email address and enter a password.

3. On the Apple ID screen, enter your Apple ID and password, then complete the setup process.

4. In the iOS Settings app, tap iCloud **B**.

5. Enter your Apple ID and password, then tap Sign In.

6. In the iCloud Settings panel, turn on the services you wish to use (**C** and **D**).

iCloud and the Apple TV

The Apple TV, the set-top box that lives near your television and allows you to access media from your iTunes library, rent movies and TV shows from the iTunes Store, and access a variety of Internet services such as Netflix, includes two iCloud services. It gives you access to your Photo Stream and to music available in iCloud using iTunes Match (see Chapter 6 for more about that).

To view your Photo Stream on your television, you'll first need to make sure the Apple TV software is updated to version 4.4 or later (the Apple TV uses a modified version of iOS with a very different user interface). Then a new item, Photo Stream, appears in the Internet menu of the Apple TV. Naturally, if you hadn't already set up the Apple TV with your Apple ID (as you would have needed to do to purchase rentals from the device), you'll need to enter it before you can view your Photo Stream. Of course, if you have more than one Apple ID, you'll need to use the one associated with your iCloud account. If you like, you can set the Photo Stream as the source for your screen saver. Or you still have the option of using one of your iPhoto albums.

Configuring iCloud on Your Mac

To activate iCloud on your Mac, you have to make sure that you have first upgraded to Mac OS X Lion 10.7.2 or later. That update added the iCloud preference pane in System Preferences.

As with an iOS device, if you previously had a MobileMe account, there are some other important considerations before you turn on iCloud on your Mac. Before you continue in this section, you should first read the "Migrating to iCloud from MobileMe" section, later in this chapter.

To set up and configure iCloud on your Mac:

1. From the Apple menu, choose System Preferences Ⓐ.

2. Click the iCloud icon.

   The iCloud preference pane appears Ⓑ.

Ⓐ Begin the iCloud setup process by opening System Preferences.

Ⓑ In the iCloud preference pane, enter the Apple ID you wish to use with iCloud, as well as its password.

To use iCloud, move your MobileMe account.

Your existing MobileMe mail, contacts, calendars and bookmarks will be automatically moved to iCloud.

Cancel   Move...

C If you already had an active MobileMe subscription, iCloud offers to begin migrating your data.

D If you didn't have a MobileMe account, choose the iCloud services you want to use from the preference pane.

3. Enter your Apple ID and password, then click Sign In.

4. (Optional) If you already had a MobileMe account, iCloud will offer to begin the migration process **C**. if you're ready to do that migration, click Move, then see the "Migrating to iCloud from MobileMe" section, later in this chapter.

5. In the iCloud preference pane, select the checkboxes next to the services you want to enable **D**.

Configuring iCloud on Your PC

If your main computer is a Windows PC, as opposed to a Mac, you can still use iCloud with it, though you only have access to a subset of the services that you would have on a Mac. On the PC, you can use iCloud for email (with a **me.com** address), contacts, calendars, and tasks (called Reminders on the iOS device), all synchronizing with Microsoft Outlook 2007 or 2010. The bookmark synchronization service works with Internet Explorer 8 or later. Your Photo Stream can also be pushed to and from your Windows PC, using folders you designate as the source and destination for iCloud photos.

Before you can use iCloud on Windows, you'll need to download the iCloud control panel from Apple's website at **http://support.apple.com/kb/DL1455**. This download will be a standard **.exe** file, which you open and install like any other Windows program.

To set up and configure iCloud on your PC:

1. Choose Start Menu > Control Panel > Network and Internet **Ⓐ**.

2. Click iCloud.

3. In the resulting iCloud control panel **Ⓑ**, select the checkboxes for the services you wish to enable.

Ⓐ Open the Network and Internet section of the Windows Control Panel to start working with the iCloud Control Panel.

Ⓑ Click the checkboxes for the iCloud services you want to use.

Migrating to iCloud from MobileMe

If you were previously a MobileMe subscriber, as part of the process of enabling iCloud on your Mac, Lion will detect your active MobileMe account and prompt you to begin the migration of your MobileMe data to iCloud. As noted earlier in this chapter, not all of the services that you enjoyed with MobileMe will survive the migration. However, MobileMe services will remain active through June 30, 2012, so services that aren't in direct conflict with iCloud, such as iWeb site hosting, the MobileMe Photo Gallery, and the contents of your iDisk, will remain active and available until the MobileMe end date.

Although I know literally dozens of people who have made the migration from MobileMe to iCloud with no problems, there's no guarantee that you'll also be one of them. Therefore, my advice is simple and clear: make sure that you have a complete backup of all your data on both your Mac and your iOS devices before you move to iCloud. Let me repeat that: have at least one good backup of every bit of your data before you start your iCloud migration. It doesn't matter if you use Apple's Time Machine, or Shirt Pocket's SuperDuper, or any other backup program, as long as you have a solid backup that won't be affected as soon as you convert to iCloud. Because I'm a stickler for backups, I made sure to update all three of my regular backup systems (yes, I use three entirely separate backup programs; yes, I know I'm a freak) immediately before I clicked the Get Started button with my MobileMe to iCloud migration.

To migrate to iCloud from MobileMe:

1. From the Apple menu, choose System Preferences.

2. Click the iCloud icon.

   The iCloud preference pane appears.

3. Enter your Apple ID and password, then click Sign In.

4. iCloud will offer to begin the migration process **A**.

5. Click Move.

   Safari will launch and begin the migration process **B**.

6. Click Get Started.

   The website will show you three informational screens that explain how your mailing calendars will be moved from MobileMe to iCloud; how you'll still be able to use Gallery, iDisk, and iWeb publishing; and which MobileMe features will no longer be available. Finally, you'll get to a screen that says "Now, upgrade your devices for iCloud." **C**.

A If you had an active MobileMe account, Lion is smart enough to recognize that and offer to begin your iCloud migration.

B In your web browser, you can begin the migration process.

C You need to confirm that all your devices are ready for iCloud.

D Once you agree to the iCloud Terms of Service and click the Move to iCloud button, the actual migration begins.

E During the migration, the browser shows you the process's progress.

F The browser shows you the alerts you'll be getting on your mobile and desktop devices to complete your move to iCloud.

7. Select the "All of the devices I want to use the iCloud are now running the required software" checkbox, then click Next.

Another couple of informational screens will appear, reminding you to have up-to-date contacts and bookmarks on one of your devices and to back up your contacts, calendars, and bookmarks before moving. Click Next to move through each of the screens, until you get to the iCloud Terms of Service screen **D**.

8. Select the "I agree to the iCloud Terms of Service" checkbox, then click Move to iCloud.

One or more screens may appear in your browser informing you of progress in moving your data from MobileMe to iCloud **E**. The final informational screen in your browser informs you that you will be getting alerts on your iOS devices, your Macs, and your Windows PCs **F**. The screen will show you what the alerts on each of those devices will look like.

continues on next page

9. Click Finished Setting Up.

It's possible that iCal will open and begin upgrading your calendars. If it doesn't, you should open it manually and allow it to upgrade the calendar data (you should open iCal at least once even if you use a third-party calendar program such as BusyMac's BusyCal, since almost all other calendar programs use iCal's data).

The iCloud preference pane should open by itself. If it does not, open it manually from System Preferences.

10. In the iCloud preference pane, select the checkbox next to each service you want to use in iCloud .

If you have more than one Mac, repeat step 10 for each computer. Ideally, you want to enable the same services on every computer.

G Select the checkboxes in the iCloud preference pane to turn on the iCloud services you wish to use.

iCloud Is Master of Your Data

In any situation where you're synchronizing data between different devices, there needs to be one master data set (also sometimes known as the *canonical* data). With MobileMe, if there was a conflict between the local copy of the data and the copy on the online service, sometimes you would get a dialog that would ask you which version of the data (on your Mac or on MobileMe) was correct, and you could choose which one to use. Not so with iCloud, which considers itself to always be the canonical data. You can even have situations (for example, if you have some duplicated calendar events) where you can delete all the events on your local machine, yet when you sync with iCloud, all those events will reappear. Sometimes, the solution is to turn off iCloud syncing on all your devices, then turn them on one by one until you get a clean set of data on all devices.

Working with Mail, Notes, and iMessages

Like its MobileMe predecessor, iCloud provides a full set of email services. There are changes (some for the better, some not so much) from MobileMe mail, but for the most part I think that iCloud email is a better product. And you can't beat the price; it's free with your iCloud account. In this chapter, we'll see how to set up your iCloud email account on both the Mac and on an iOS device, and manage that mail on the iCloud website.

As part of Apple's Mail program and the iOS Notes app, you also have the ability to create notes that will sync between your devices via iCloud. You'll see how to deal with notes on both platforms.

One of the new features in iCloud is iMessages, which allows you to send text messages to other people on iOS devices with iCloud accounts, and without incurring phone carrier messaging charges. iMessage is integrated into the Messages iOS app, and we'll see how it works and its limitations.

Setting up iCloud Mail Accounts on Your Mac

One of the benefits of every iCloud account is a free **@me.com** email address (if you previously had a **mac.com** address, that serves as an alias to the **me.com** address). All iCloud email accounts use the IMAP email protocol, so messages are saved on the server, and you can read, reply to, and mark your email as read from any device. Because IMAP is a standard mail protocol, you can use many different email programs, on many different computing platforms, to work with your mail. You're certainly not locked into just using Apple devices.

Because messages are saved on the server, the amount of space your email takes up counts against the free 5 GB of storage space you get with your iCloud account.

When email arrives in your iCloud email account, the email is also automatically pushed to your iOS devices, so your mail picture is the same whether you're on a Mac or on a mobile device.

Dealing with how to use the Apple Mail program on the Mac (to send and receive mail, for example) is outside the scope of this book; instead, in this chapter I'm going to focus on showing you how to set up Mail with your iCloud account, depending on if you were a previous Mail user or not. Again, since your iCloud email account is just like any other IMAP account, you can set it up on almost any email program, just follow the maker's instructions for setting up an account. I will go into working with many aspects of mail using the iCloud website, which can be accessed from any web browser; see "Working with Mail on the iCloud Website" later in this chapter.

MobileMe Mail Features Missing from iCloud Mail

There are a few things you could do with MobileMe mail that you can't do with iCloud mail. First of all, iCloud uses the more modern IMAP email protocol exclusively, so you can't retrieve your messages with the POP email protocol. In my opinion, that's not necessarily a bad thing, but it does limit flexibility for some people.

MobileMe email allowed you to use Apple's mail servers, but you could change the From address of your messages, so if you had previously had a long-standing email address (on, for example, your own domain), you could use MobileMe as your mail provider and still send email that apparently came from your other address. For example, I could previously send mail from **tn@negrino.com** via the MobileMe servers. That's no longer possible; you must now use your **.me** account (or legacy **.mac** account) as the From address. If this ability is important to you, it is available from other free email providers, such as Google's Gmail.

One minor change is that MobileMe allowed up to five email aliases, and iCloud only allows three aliases. An alias is an email address that points to another address; for example, you could have a **workmail@me.com** alias that you pick up on your main **.me** account. You can also use an alias address to help filter your mail using mail rules.

A If you've never used Mail on your Mac before, setting up your first account welcomes you to the program.

B Mail checks to make sure that the email address and password you entered were valid.

To set up your iCloud email account in Apple Mail (if you haven't used Mail before):

1. On your Mac, choose Applications > Mail.

   The Welcome to Mail Screen appears **A**.

2. You'll be prompted for the Full Name, the Email Address, and the Password. Enter these, then click Create.

   Mail checks to see if the email account exists, and if so signs you in and the Account Summary screen appears **B**.

3. (Optional) If you also want to set up your Contacts and Calendars to work with iCloud, select those checkboxes next to Also set up. I recommend that you do this.

4. Click Create.

   Mail opens, displaying the mail window **C**.

Toolbar   Message list   Message area   Search box

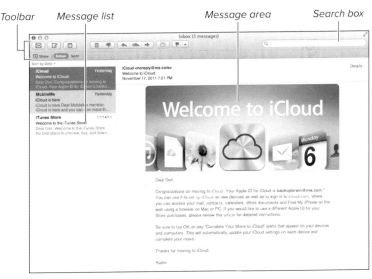

C The Mail application window on the Mac, in its default configuration.

To set up your iCloud email account in Apple Mail (if you've used Mail before):

1. On your Mac, choose Applications > Mail.

2. In Mail, choose Mail > Preferences > Accounts.

   The Accounts pane appears .

3. At the lower left corner of the pane, click the plus button.

   The Add Account pane appears .

4. Enter the Full Name, the Email Address, and the Password, then click Create.

   Mail checks to see if the email account exists, and if so signs you in and the Account Summary screen appears **B**.

5. (Optional) If you also want to set up your Contacts and Calendars to work with iCloud, select those checkboxes next to Also set up. I recommend that you do this.

6. Click Create.

7. Close the Mail Preferences window.

D If you already have an email address in Mail, you begin adding a new one in the Accounts pane of Mail's Preferences.

E Enter your name, email address, and password on the Add Accounts screen.

Setting up Mail Accounts on Your iOS Device

On the Mac, you set up new email accounts in the Mail program, but that's not the case on iOS. Instead, you use the Settings app. You can have more than one mail account on your iOS device, and you can even have more than one iCloud account (if, for example, you have separate iCloud accounts for personal and school, or home and work). In this example, we'll focus on setting up an iCloud account, but the steps you take are much the same for any email provider.

To set up a mail account on an iOS device:

1. Tap Settings, then scroll down to Mail, Contacts, Calendars **Ⓐ**, then tap that.

   The Mail, Contacts, Calendars screen appears **Ⓑ**.

2. Tap Add Account.

3. On the resulting Add Account screen **Ⓒ**, tap iCloud from the list of email providers.

   If you choose a different provider, you may have to enter a bit more information. For example, if you choose Gmail, you'll be asked for your name, email address, password, and a description of the account.

   continues on next page

Ⓐ Begin setting up a new email account in the Settings app.

Ⓑ Tap Add Account to start the new account process.

Ⓒ In iOS 5, there are a variety of preset email providers. In this case, we want iCloud.

4. Enter your Apple ID and password, then tap the Next button .

On this screen, if you don't already have an Apple ID, you have the opportunity to get one by tapping the Get a Free Apple ID button at the bottom of the screen. That takes you through creating an Apple ID process.

5. The device verifies your Apple ID and password, then brings you to the iCloud settings screen , which allows you to turn iCloud services on or off for your device. As you can see, most settings are turned on by default. Choose the settings you wish to enable on that particular device, then tap Save.

The device will return to the Mail, Contacts, Calendars screen, showing the new account 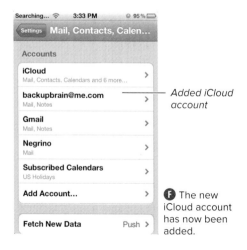. If you have more than one iCloud account, the second one will appear showing the email address associated with that account as the name of the account.

D Enter your Apple ID and password, then tap the Next button.

E Because we're setting up an iCloud account, you can choose which iCloud services to enable.

Added iCloud account

F The new iCloud account has now been added.

G Tapping the Account name allows you to change its description.

6. (Optional) If you want to rename the additional account to something other than the email address, tap the account name on the Mail, Contacts, Calendars screen, tap the Account field G, and in the resulting Account screen, change the Description H. Tap the Done button. When you are returned to the Mail, Contacts, Calendars screen, things may not appear to have initially changed, but leaving that screen and returning shows the change was made I.

H Type the new description for the account.

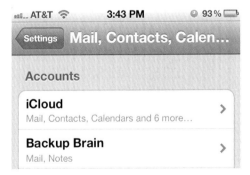

I Back in the Mail, Contacts, Calendars screen, the updated description appears.

Working with Notes

Notes on an iOS device (in the Notes app) or in Apple Mail on the Mac are like yellow sticky notes in the real world. You can use them for reminders, general notes, pretty much whatever you want in terms of small snippets of text. Notes that you create or edit on one iOS device will, if you have it set up, automatically synchronize to your other iOS devices, and to Apple Mail on the Mac.

You can have different notes associated with different accounts, depending on whether or not the account supports notes. Most email accounts from many different email providers do, as iCloud treats Notes as a special sort of email. So you can use notes in iCloud, and synchronize them with most IMAP accounts.

In Apple Mail, notes appear in the sidebar under the Reminders section Ⓐ. If you have more than one account enabled for Notes, then the accounts will all appear in the sidebar separately.

On an iOS device, you create Notes by typing in the Notes app, or if you're using a Siri-enabled device, you can dictate notes to Siri, and they will appear in the Notes app. On your mobile device, you need to first set the default account destination for your notes.

On the iCloud website, you can only view Notes; you can't create new ones or edit existing ones.

Ⓐ Notes are integrated into Apple's Mail program on the Mac.

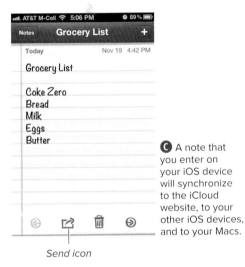

B Choose the font and default account you want to use in the Notes app on your iOS device.

C A note that you enter on your iOS device will synchronize to the iCloud website, to your other iOS devices, and to your Macs.

Send icon

D You can use Printopia to AirPrint-enable any printer on your local network.

To configure Notes on an iOS device:

1. Tap Settings > Notes.

2. On the Notes settings screen **B**, choose the font you want to use for your notes, then tap Default Account.

    The screen changes to show the different accounts that can accept Notes.

3. Tap the account you want to use as your default Notes account. A checkmark will appear next to that account name.

4. Press the iOS device's Home button to save your choice.

To create Notes on an iOS device:

1. Tap Notes.

2. Tap the plus button at the upper right of the screen.

    A new Note form appears. Type the note **C**.

TIP To delete the note, tap the Trash icon at the bottom of the note.

TIP You can also email or print a note by tapping the Send icon at the bottom of the note. In order to print, you must have an AirPrint-capable printer available. AirPrint allows an iOS device to print wirelessly over Wi-Fi.

TIP Though AirPrint is normally a hardware feature in a printer, some clever software, Ecamm Network's (www.ecamm.com) $20 Printopia 2, installs as a preference pane on a Mac **D** and then allows any printer your Mac can use to be accessed by AirPrint on your iOS devices. This doesn't just work with Notes; it works with any app on your iOS device that can print, such as Pages or Keynote. You can also use Printopia to "print" a PDF to your Mac, Dropbox's Dropbox, or Evernote's Evernote (if you subscribe to those services).

To work with Notes in Apple Mail:

1. In Mail's sidebar, click the account that you created the note in, then select the note in the message list.

   The contents of the note appear in the message area **E**.

2. Double-click an existing note in the message list to open it in a new window for editing **F**.

   or

   To create a new note, choose File> New Note, or click the Compose new note button in the toolbar **G**.

   or

   To delete a note, select it in the message list and then press the Delete key or choose Edit > Delete.

TIP Annoyingly, notes you create on iOS devices don't just show up in the sidebar under Reminders in Apple Mail; by default, they also show up in your Inbox. If this makes as little sense to you as it does to me (the Inbox is for mail, darn it), choose Mail > Preferences > Accounts, then click the account whose behavior you want to change in the list on the left of the window. Click the Mailbox Behaviors tab, then deselect the Show notes in Inbox checkbox.

E On the Mac, an iOS Note appears much the same as it does on the mobile device.

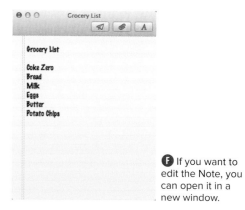

F If you want to edit the Note, you can open it in a new window.

Get new messages   Compose new message   Compose new note

G You can also create new Notes in Mail.

H You can view Notes in the Mail application on the iCloud website, but you can't add new Notes or edit them.

To view Notes on the iCloud website:

1. Log in to the iCloud website.

2. If necessary, from the homepage, click the Mail icon. If you are in another application, click the iCloud icon in the upper left corner of the window, then click the Mail icon.

3. In the website's Mail application, under Folders in the sidebar, click Notes, then in the message list, click the note you wish to view **H**.

   On the iCloud website, you can only view and not edit or create Notes.

Working with Mail on the iCloud Website

If you are familiar with Mail on the Mac, you'll immediately feel at home in the Mail application on the iCloud website. It's designed to resemble the desktop application fairly closely **Ⓐ**.

Like the desktop application, you'll find a Mailboxes and Folders list; a message list; a message area; a search box; and a toolbar that allows you to create and work with messages. The Actions icon, which

looks like a gear in the upper right corner of the window, allows you to customize the behavior of the web application and apply actions to individual messages.

If you're wondering about spam, I'm happy to report that Apple has generally got a pretty good set of spam filters. On my iCloud account (and before that on my MobileMe account) spam rarely gets through to my Inbox. And from a security standpoint, iCloud Mail uses the HTTPS protocol, which encrypts all traffic to and from the website; it's the same level of security used for online shopping.

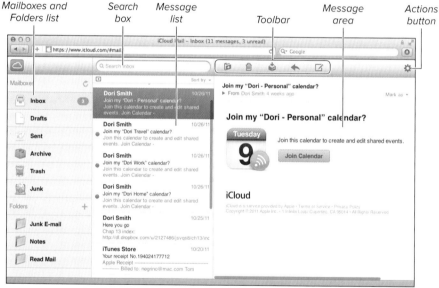

Mailboxes and Folders list   Search box   Message list   Toolbar   Message area   Actions button

Ⓐ Mail on the iCloud website looks a good bit like Mail on the Mac.

Resize arrow   Refresh messages   Hide/Show Mailboxes

B Drag the double-headed arrow right or left to change the width of the Mailboxes and Folders list.

C Clicking a message in the message list shows its contents in the message area.

Using the Mail Application

Besides working with messages, mailboxes, and folders, Mail lets you customize it so that it works the way you want it to.

To resize or hide the Mailboxes and Folders list or message list:

To resize the width of the Mailboxes and Folders list, point to the bar between that list and the message list. The cursor will change to a double-headed arrow **B**. Click and drag to the right or left to resize.

or

To resize the width of the message area, point to the bar between the message list and the message area. The cursor will change to a double-headed arrow. Click and drag to the right or left to resize.

or

To hide the Mailboxes and Folders list altogether, click the Hide/Show mailboxes toggle button. Click it again to display the list again.

To view messages:

1. In the Mailboxes and Folders list, click the mailbox or folder whose contents you wish to view.

    The contents of the message list will change to display the contents of the selected mailbox or folder.

2. In the message list, click the message you wish to view to show its contents in the message area **C**.

    or

    In the message list, double-click the message you wish to view to open the message in a new window.

Working with Email

When working with email, you want to receive it, file it, write replies to emails you get, sort it so that you can see your message list in some comprehensible fashion, and search your email to find mail that matches a particular keyword. The iCloud Mail application handles all these needs with aplomb.

Many of these features use the toolbar at the top of the message list **D**. Let's take a closer look at the functions of each of the toolbar icons.

- **Move to Folder** takes a selected message and moves it to one of the other folders in the Mailboxes and Folders list.

- **Delete** moves the selected message to the Trash mailbox. Messages in the Trash are automatically deleted after 30 days. You can also immediately delete the contents of the Trash mailbox by clicking the Actions icon in the upper right corner of the window and choosing Empty Trash from the pop-up menu.

- **Archive** moves the selected message to the Archive mailbox. Each account you have has its own Archive mailbox. Use Archive when you want to move something out of the Inbox—to get it out of your way—but you still want to be able to easily search for that item.

- **Reply, Reply All, Forward** allows you to reply to an incoming message, reply to all addressees for that message, or forward that message to a new recipient.

- **Compose** allows you to create a new message.

Move to Folder Delete Archive Reply, Reply All, Forward Compose

D You'll use the toolbar to do a lot of your work with email messages.

E You'll compose new messages in the New Message window.

To get new messages:

When you first sign in, iCloud checks for new messages automatically, but if you're working in the application for a while and you want to recheck manually, click the refresh icon at the top of the Mailboxes and Folders list **B**. You can tell a message is unread because it has a blue dot next to it.

To compose new mail:

1. In the toolbar, click the Compose button.

   A new message window opens **E**.

2. Begin typing the recipient's name in the To field. If the recipient is in your Contact list, a pop-up menu with matching addresses will appear. Choose the recipient you want from the pop-up menu, then press the Return key.

3. (Optional) To add additional recipients to the To field, click the blue plus in a circle icon at the right edge of the To field, then choose additional recipients.

4. (Optional) To add CC recipients, add them to the CC field.

5. Enter the email subject in the Subject field.

6. Type the message body.

continues on next page

7. (Optional) You can use the Style toolbar to style text in your message by changing the font, font size, font color, adding bold, italic, or underlined text, changing the justification, adding a bulleted or numbered list, changing the text indent, adding hyperlinks, or adding file attachments.

   By default, iCloud mail is HTML mail, which supports this sort of text styling.

8. When you are done composing your message, click the Send button.

F The pop-up menu in the toolbar gives you your choices of Reply, Reply All, or Forward.

TIP If you click the Save button at the right edge of the Style toolbar, it saves the message as a draft, and files a copy of the message in the Drafts mailbox. You can then close the message window without sending the message and return to it later to finish it up.

To reply to or forward mail:

1. Click to select a message in the message list.

2. In the toolbar, click the Reply, Reply All, Forward button.

   A pop-up menu appears with the various choices **F**.

3. Pick the choice you want from the pop-up menu, and a new message window appears, by default with the contents of the message you're replying to already in the message body as a quotation.

4. (Optional) If you are forwarding the message, enter the new recipient in the To field.

5. Enter your reply, or a message you want to add if you are forwarding the original mail, then click the Send button.

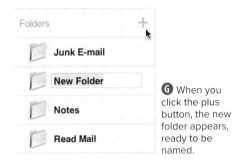

Folders

Junk E-mail

New Folder

Notes

Read Mail

G When you click the plus button, the new folder appears, ready to be named.

To file mail:

1. In the message list, click to select the message you want to file.

2. Do one of the following:

   ▸ Click the Move to Folder button in the toolbar, then choose one of the folders from the resulting pop-up menu.

   ▸ Drag the message from the message list to one of the folders in the Mailboxes and Folders list.

   ▸ Click the Archive button in the toolbar to move the selected message to the Archive mailbox.

TIP You can move multiple contiguous messages in the message list by clicking the first message, holding down the Shift key, then clicking the last message. All messages in between will be selected. Then you can drag them or use one of the toolbar buttons to move them as a group. If you want to move noncontiguous messages in the message list, hold down the Command key and click the messages you wish to move before dragging or using the toolbar buttons.

To add a new folder:

1. At the top of the Folders section of the Mailboxes and Folders list, click the plus button.

   A new folder will appear in the Folder list, ready to be named **G**.

2. Type the name of the new folder, then click anywhere else in the window.

TIP You can drag one folder into another to make it a subfolder. To move a folder out of another folder, drag it to the Folders header in the list.

To delete a folder:

1. Click to select the folder in the Mailboxes and Folders list.

2. Click the Actions button at the upper
   right corner of the window, then from
   the resulting pop-up menu, choose
   Delete Folder.

   iCloud will ask you if you're sure
   you want to delete the folder and its
   contents.

3. Click Delete.

> **TIP** Remember that because your iCloud
> email account is synchronized across all your
> devices, folders that you create or delete on
> the website will also appear or disappear on
> the rest of your devices.

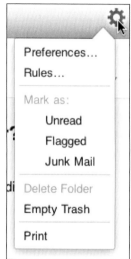

H You mark
messages from the
Actions pop-up menu.

To mark messages:

1. Click to select one or more messages
   from the message list.

2. Click the Actions button in the upper
   right corner of the window.

3. From the resulting pop-up menu **H**,
   choose Unread, Flagged, or Junk Mail
   in the Mark as section.

   Choosing Unread returns a message's
   state to unread if you've already looked
   at it. Choosing Flagged adds a flag icon
   to the message, which you can later
   use for sorting purposes. And choosing Junk Mail moves the message to
   the Junk folder.

> **TIP** If you've accidentally moved mail to the
> Junk mailbox, you can click a message in the
> message list for that mailbox and the menu
> choice in the Actions pop-up menu will change
> to Not Junk Mail. Choosing that moves the
> message back to your Inbox.

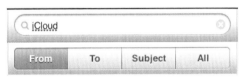

❶ Choose your Sort by criteria.

❶ When you click in the Search box, you have the option of narrowing your search by one of four criteria.

To sort messages:

At the top of the message list, click the Sort by button. From the resulting pop-up menu **❶**, choose how you want to sort the contents of the message list. Your choices are by Date, From, Subject, Unread, or Flagged. You can also choose Ascending or Descending order.

The message display in the Message list changes according to the sort order you picked.

To search for messages:

1. In the Mailboxes and Folders list, click the mailbox or folder that you wish to search.

   Unfortunately, you can't search your entire mail system at once.

2. Click in the Search box, and enter your search term.

3. (Optional) When you click in the Search box, an additional toolbar appears allowing you to narrow your search to the From, To, Subject, or All fields in the messages **❶**. Click one of these toolbar buttons to narrow your search.

4. Press the Return key.

   iCloud displays the matching messages in the message list.

TIP Although you can't search all of your Mailboxes and Folders simultaneously, iCloud does allow you to search in the contents of the messages, which is an improvement over MobileMe.

To add contacts from incoming mail:

1. In a message list, click to select the message with a contact you wish to add to your iCloud Contacts list.

2. In the message, click the sender's email address, and then click Add in the resulting popover .

To print a message:

1. Click to select a message from the message list.

2. From the Actions pop-up menu, choose Print.

   The message will open in a new window and the Print dialog for the system you're working on will appear. Choose the printing options, then click Print.

🅚 Click an email address in an incoming message to add that person to your iCloud Contacts list.

L The iCloud Mail application has many useful preferences.

M Choose the preferences you want from the General tab.

Working with Mail Preferences

The Actions menu has a Preferences choice, which leads you to a window with five tabs: General, Addresses, Composing, Rules, and Vacation **L**. In the sections below, we'll go through each of these Preferences tabs.

To set General preferences:

1. Click the Actions button, then choose Preferences.

2. Click the General tab to show the general preferences **M**.

3. Choose one or more of the following:

   ▶ **Load images in HTML messages** shows you all images in messages. If this is unchecked, you won't see images in HTML mail unless you click a Load Images button in the message.

   ▶ **Show all folders at login** shows you all the folders in the list when you sign in to iCloud mail. If you have a lot of folders, you might want to turn this off so that only the top level folders appear in the list and you don't have to scroll your browser window to see everything.

   ▶ **Show message previews** tells the iCloud mail application to show the first couple of lines of each message in the message list. This is one of the default choices, and I find it extremely useful.

continues on next page

- **Forward my email to** allows you to send all of your incoming email to another address. If you have an assistant who also monitors your mail, you might want to use this option. You'll need to select the checkbox and enter the forwarding email address.

- **Delete messages after forwarding** erases your incoming messages after they have been forwarded to the alternate email address.

- **Save sent messages in** allows you to pick the folder where sent messages are automatically filed from the pop-up menu. This is off by default, which makes no sense to me. Why wouldn't you want copies of message that you send? The only reason I can think of is that an outgoing messages count against your iCloud storage quota.

- **Move deleted messages to** allows you to choose the folder where deleted messages are sent, usually the Trash folder. A message moved to the Trash is automatically and permanently deleted after 30 days.

You can add new email addresses in the Addresses tab.

To set Addresses preferences:

1. Click the Actions button, then choose Preferences.

2. Click the Addresses tab .

3. Click the **Add an alias** link to add an email alias (iCloud allows you to have up to three aliases), which is a secondary **me.com** address that points to your main **me.com** address. Email sent to one of the aliases is delivered to your main account. Here's how it might work in practice: my main iCloud account address is **negrino@me.com**. But I might also create an alias of **tomnegrino@me.com**.

4. In the Alias field, add the alias you want to you (you don't need to enter the **me.com** part).

5. Click OK. The site checks to see if the alias is already in use; if it is, the alias you asked for will be rejected, and you'll be prompted for a new one.

6. Click Done.

   The new alias appears in the Addresses Preferences pane.

TIP You can use an alias as the From address in outgoing mail, if you want to keep a particular email address private. Replies will go to the alias.

To set Composing preferences:

1. Click the Actions button, then choose Preferences.

2. Click the Composing tab .

3. Choose one or more of the following:

   ▸ **Include original message when replying** includes the entire message that you're replying to as a quote. I usually prefer to edit the quote down to just the essentials, because I think that it makes email conversations easier to read.

   ▸ **Show Bcc field** makes the blind carbon copy field always appear in the Add Message window.

   ▸ **Send outgoing messages using Unicode (UTF-8)** tells Mail to allow your messages to contain non-Latin characters, such as Hebrew, Arabic, or Chinese.

   ▸ **Send new messages from** sets Mail to automatically use the email address or email alias you choose from the pop-up menu for new messages.

   ▸ **Add a signature to your outbound mail** allows you to append a message to the end of every mail that you create. For example, you might want to include your contact information.

TIP Signatures that you set up on the iCloud website don't synchronize with email signatures from Mail on the Mac or on your iOS devices, and vice versa.

Ⓞ You can fine-tune the way you send email in the Composing section of Preferences.

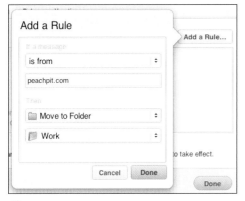

P iCloud doesn't start with any Rules. You must add them.

Q Choose the criteria you want for your Rule in the popover.

To set Rules:

1. Click the Actions button, then choose Preferences.

2. Click the Rules tab **P**.

   Mail rules run on the server and can automatically run actions on incoming messages. You set some criteria, and then an action to automatically occur when that criterion is met. Let's say that I have a mail folder called Family. I can set up a rule so that all incoming email from my wife automatically gets routed to the Family folder.

3. Click the **Add a Rule** button.

4. In the resulting popover, set the If criterion and the Then action to be taken **Q**. You don't have a lot of choices here; in the If section, you can trigger an action on the From, To, CC, or Subject fields. In the Then section, your choices are Move to Folder, Move to Trash, or Forward to a different email address.

5. Click Done.

   The rule that you created appears in the Rules tab of Preferences.

TIP The Rules ability of the iCloud website is fairly rudimentary; although you can set up multiple rules, you can't set up multiple criteria or actions for a single rule, which makes it much less powerful than the Rules ability in Apple Mail, Gmail, and other systems.

To set Vacation preferences:

1. Click the Actions button, then choose Preferences.

2. Click the Vacation tab 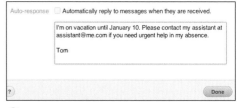.

3. If you want to send out a vacation message, select the **Automatically reply to messages when they are received** checkbox.

4. Enter a vacation message in the text field, then click Done.

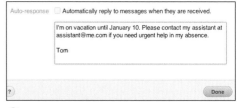

Auto-response ☐ Automatically reply to messages when they are received.

I'm on vacation until January 10. Please contact my assistant at assistant@me.com if you need urgent help in my absence.

Tom

? Done

R Enter your Vacation message.

Sending iMessages

SMS text messaging has been around for a long time, and for just as long, the cellular carriers have been making money hand over fist on the feature. It's widely reported that text messaging costs carriers virtually nothing, since the texts are sent over control channels used for network maintenance. At best, carrier costs have been estimated as 1/1000th of a cent per text message. But they cost *you* a *lot*: in October 2011, *Macworld* magazine compared unlimited text messaging plans for the U.S. carriers (AT&T, Verizon, and Sprint) and found that carriers were charging $20 for unlimited text messaging, or you can pay-as-you-go for $.20 per text message. Anyway you look at it, that's not a good deal. If you look at MMS (text messages that include pictures or video), the pay-as-you-go rate is $.25 or $.30, depending on the carrier. It's safe to say that there is an obscene amount of profit in the text messaging business.

iCloud and iOS 5 include a free service called iMessage that allow you to send unlimited messages between you and anyone else who is also using a device with iOS 5 (an iPhone, iPad, or iPod touch) and an iCloud account. You can send photos, videos, locations, and contacts, as well as texts. If you have more than one iOS device, you can start a conversation on one device and continue it on another.

With iMessage, you can send a message to more than one person at a time, and if you do, a reply from one person is seen by everyone on the list. Unlike regular text messages, when your message appears on the recipient's iOS device, you get a delivery confirmation, and you can tell with a text balloon when the other person is typing a reply.

Of course, if you are signed up for a text plan with your carrier, you can still send text messages over the cellular network. From your standpoint, there's almost no difference between the two (except for cost, convenience, and better performance), because both standard texting and iMessage are integrated into the iOS Messages app.

To send an iMessage:

1. On an iOS device, tap Messages.

2. In the Messages app, either choose a previous recipient, or tap the New Message button in the upper right-hand corner of the screen.

3. (Optional) If you're sending to a new recipient, enter their name in the To field.

4. If your recipient is eligible for an iMessage, the text entry field will faintly show iMessage .

5. Enter your iMessage, then tap the Send button.

A You can tell you're in an iMessage conversation because it says iMessage in the text field, and because of the text balloons with the blue background.

TIP You can tell the difference between an iMessage and regular text messaging in the Messages app easily, because your outgoing text balloons will have a blue background for people who can accept iMessages. For people with whom you are doing regular text messaging, your outgoing text balloon will have a green background (the color of U.S. money, Apple? Real subtle).

TIP Besides the delivery confirmation you get when the recipient gets your iMessage, you can also get a receipt when they actually *read* the message. This seems just a bit creepy, until you think about it; it can be nice to know that not only did you send that text to your spouse about picking up some milk on the way home, but that the message isn't just waiting forlornly in their pocket or purse. To turn on this receipt feature, choose **Settings** > **Messages**, then turn on **Send Read Receipts**.

TIP iMessage is tied not just to mobile phone numbers, as regular SMS messages are; it's also attached to email addresses. So any email address that iCloud knows about can receive an iMessage. That's how you can use iMessage with the iPad or iPod touch, which don't have mobile phone numbers. In the Receive At section of **Settings** > **Messages**, you can specify what email addresses can be used for iMessages. These addresses don't have to be the ones associated with your Apple ID; if you want, you can use any valid email address, not just a .me or .mac address.

3

Working with Contacts

The people and companies that you deal with are stored in your Mac's Address Book, and in the Contacts app in iOS and iCloud. Using iCloud, changes that you make on any of your devices get synchronized immediately to the rest of your devices. So, for example, if you change a contact's address, phone number, email address, or other information in Address Book on your Mac, those changes will be pushed automatically and effortlessly to your mobile devices, and to any other Macs that share your iCloud account. The reverse is also true; changes made on a mobile device are synchronized back to your Macs over the air, whether it be via Wi-Fi or the cellular network.

In addition to the changes you can make to contacts on your Macs and mobile devices, you can also manage contacts using the Contacts application on the iCloud website. In this chapter, we'll focus mainly on using the website for contact management.

In This Chapter

Searching, Adding, and Editing Contacts in iCloud

To begin working with your contacts, go to the iCloud website **Ⓐ**, sign in if necessary, and click on the Contacts application **Ⓑ**, which closely resembles the Address Book application on the Mac.

You can view any contact by scrolling through the All Contacts list, or by clicking on one of the letter tabs at the left side of the window to jump you to that part of the alphabet. Clicking to select a contact in the list gives you that contact's details on the right side of the window.

Besides simply finding things manually, you can also search your Contacts, add new ones, and edit existing contacts through the website application.

Ⓐ Choose the Contacts application from the iCloud website.

Ⓑ The iCloud Contacts web application closely resembles the Mac Address Book application.

All Contacts

smith

ICE

Dori **Smith**

Marie **Smith**

Sean **Smith**

C Typing in the Search field immediately narrows the list of found contacts.

To search contacts:

In the Search field at the upper left part of the Contacts application, type all or part of any item in the contact's information. The Contacts List immediately shrinks to show the search results **C**. To clear the Search field, click the round button with an X in it.

The search term will be highlighted in each found contact's entry.

TIP Note that iCloud searches through all of the information in your Contacts data, not just names. So you can do useful things like search for all of the people with Gmail addresses, or search through your contact's Notes field.

TIP Some of the information in the contact record is clickable. To send the contact an email message, click an email address. Similarly, URLs are clickable, opening a new browser window. To display a map of the contact's address, click a real-world address, which opens another window showing you the address in Google Maps **D**.

D Clicking a physical address in the Contacts application opens another browser window, displaying that location in Google Maps.

To add a new contact:

1. On the iCloud website, click the Plus button at the bottom of the Contacts list.

   or

   From the Action menu (the gear icon at the bottom of the Contacts list), choose New Contact **Ⓔ**.

2. In the resulting Edit Contact screen **Ⓕ**, enter the information for your new contact.

3. Click Done.

   iCloud saves your work, and will shortly synchronize it to the rest of your iCloud-enabled devices.

Ⓔ The Action pop-up menu at the bottom of the Contacts list gives you a variety of choices.

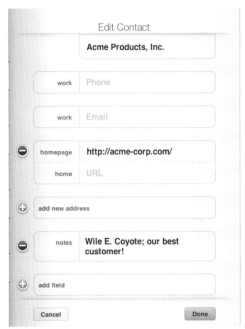

Ⓕ A new contact has a variety of fields already laid out for you, but you can also add custom fields by clicking the Add Field button at the bottom of the contact record.

Related People allow you to connect other people and their relationship to a particular contact.

To edit contacts:

1. Find the contact you wish to change in the Contacts List, then click on it to select it.

2. Click Edit.

3. Make the changes you need, then click Done.

TIP When you're editing contacts, you can add a new optional field called **Related People. This new field lets you specify other people who are related to the person whose contact record you are editing. For example, if you choose to add a Related People field, you can choose the relationship (Father, Mother, Spouse, Child, and so on) from a pop-up menu, then enter the name of the related person in the field** **. If you have a iPhone 4S or other device that uses Siri, make sure to add one or more of these fields to your own contact card, so Siri knows what you mean when you say things like "Text my wife that I'll be late."**

To delete a contact:

1. Find the contact you wish to delete in the Contacts List, then click on it to select it.

2. Press Delete or Backspace.

You'll get a confirmation dialog asking if you really want to delete that record. Click Delete.

TIP You can use the Shift or Command keys to select multiple contacts in the list before you delete them.

Working with Contact Groups

A contact group is a list of one or more contacts. You can create them on the Mac Address Book, or on the iCloud Contacts application. These are handy for things like grouping similar people together. For example, I have a Friends group in my Mac Address Book, with the names of five friends to whom I often share interesting email. In Mail on the Mac, all I have to do to address a message to all five people is to enter the name of the group in the email's To field.

While you can create and work with contact groups on the Mac's Address Book, and those groups synchronize to iOS devices, oddly, the Mail app in iOS 5 doesn't allow you to use Groups to address mail. You also can't add, edit, or delete groups on a mobile device. It's as though the feature is there as the foundation for a future revision of iOS.

You can work with groups on the iCloud website, however. Let's take a look at how to do that.

A Click the Groups ribbon at the right of the window to change to Groups mode.

B The Groups list appears on the left side of the window.

To work in Groups mode:

1. At the top of the Contacts List, click the Groups ribbon **A**.

   The display will switch to showing just your groups on the left **B**. The All Contacts group is always at the top of the list, which displays your entire Contacts list on the right side of the window.

2. Click a Group name to display its members on the right side of the window **C**.

   continues on next page

C Clicking the name of the group displays its members on the right side of the window.

3. Do one or more of the following:

- ▶ Add a group by clicking the Plus button at the bottom of the Groups pane.

- ▶ Remove a group by clicking the Edit button at the bottom of the Groups pane, then click the minus icon next to the group you want to delete. As usual, you'll get a confirmation dialog. Click Delete.

- ▶ Rename a group by clicking the Edit button at the bottom of the Groups pane, then change the group's name. Click Done to save your changes.

- ▶ Add a member to a group by clicking the All Contacts group, then drag a contact into another group to add it to that group. It's okay if a contact is in more than one group, so you can drag names from one group to another.

- ▶ Remove a member from a group by first selecting the group and then the contact you want to remove. Press the Backspace or Delete key. Interestingly, you won't get a confirmation dialog when you delete a contact from any group other than All Contacts.

4. When you're done working with groups, click the individual ribbon at the top of the window.

A The Action menu allows you to work further with your contacts.

Tom **Negrino**

B The silhouette icon denotes your own contact card.

Using the Action Menu

The Action menu at the bottom of the iCloud Contacts application's window gives you a variety of additional commands **A**.

- **Preferences** will be covered in the next section.

- Choose **New Contact** to add a contact to the Contacts list. This is the equivalent of clicking the Plus button at the bottom of the Contacts list.

- **Select All** lets you easily select all of your contacts at once.

- **Delete** allows you to remove one or more selected contacts. It's the equivalent of selecting a contact and pressing Backspace or Delete.

- **Print** allows you to print the selected contact cards. You will get the usual system printing dialog, so you can adjust the print settings to your liking.

- **Make This My Card** allows you to specify your own contact card. When you do this, Contacts marks it with the silhouette icon **B**. Mac OS X and iOS uses this information to identify you for mail, contacts, and more.

- **Refresh Contacts** forces the website to reload your contact data if you've updated contacts on another device, and those changes haven't yet appeared on the iCloud website.

Setting iCloud Contact Preferences

Choosing Preferences from the Action menu allows you to set some general behavior of the iCloud Contacts application.

To set Contact preferences:

1. Choose Preferences from the Action menu.

   The preferences dialog appears 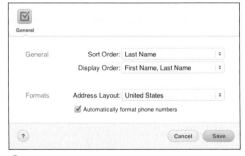.

2. Choose one or more of the following:

   ▸ In the **Sort Order** pop-up menu, choose either First Name or Last Name to tell iCloud how you want contacts sorted.

   ▸ In the **Display Order** pop-up menu, choose either First Name, Last Name or Last Name, First Name to tell iCloud how you want names to appear in the list.

   ▸ In the **Address Layout** pop-up menu, choose a country name to determine how addresses are shown.

   ▸ Choose **Automatically Format Phone Numbers** to tell iCloud to automatically format telephone numbers in the format appropriate for the country you chose in the Address Layout pop-up menu.

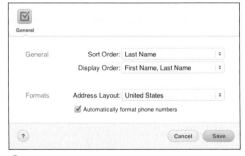

Ⓐ The Preferences dialog allows you to choose how the iCloud Contacts application sorts and displays your contacts.

Working with Calendars and Reminders

One of the best—and incredibly useful—features of iCloud is its ability to keep your calendar events and reminders in the cloud, automatically synchronizing them among all your devices. Imagine you've just finished an appointment at the dentist, and the receptionist asks to set up your next date. Whipping out your iPhone, you enter the next appointment into the Calendar app, and in a moment, that appointment appears on the rest of your devices.

Similarly, iCloud can create synchronized reminders for things you need to do. With the iOS 5 Reminders app, you can even set a reminder to appear only when you arrive at a particular geographical location.

But probably the most useful feature of iCloud calendaring is that you can share your calendars with family, friends, and colleagues. So when your daughter adds her soccer practice to the family shared calendar, it appears on the rest of the family's schedule as well.

In This Chapter

Setting up Calendars

You begin with calendars in iCloud by creating them, either in iCal or in the iOS Calendar app. You can also create calendars on the iCloud website 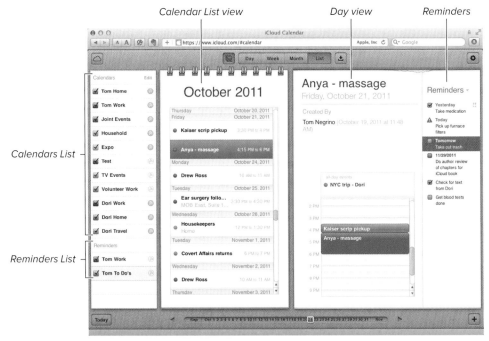, which I'll discuss later in this chapter.

There's one important concept to get when you start managing your schedule and to-dos with iCloud. There are two kinds of items that iCloud deals with:

- **Events** are items that appear in the body of your calendar views. They will appear in the Day, Week, Month, and List views. They always have dates and times associated with them (though sometimes the associated time is "all-day").

- **Reminders** are to-do items. They work differently than they did with MobileMe, in that Reminders "calendars" now appear in a separate Reminders section in the Calendar List in iCal and the iCloud website (as such, a group of reminders is now properly called a Reminder List, not a Calendar) and you work with them in the iOS Reminders app, rather than with the Calendar app. Reminders don't appear in the calendar views; you have to show the Reminders pane in iCal and the iCloud website to see them. Reminders may have a date and time associated with them, but don't have to. Unlike Events, you can also set a Priority (None, Low, Medium, High) for a Reminder. Using a feature called "geofencing," they can also be

Calendar List view   Day view   Reminders

Calendars List

Reminders List

A The Calendar application on the iCloud website has a variety of calendar views.

Were You Using or Sharing MobileMe Calendars?

Before you do anything with iCloud calendars (or actually, before you move to iCloud at all), it's good to know two things: First, your MobileMe calendars will be moved to iCloud as part of the migration process. It's a one-way trip; once you move your calendars to iCloud, there's no going back. Second, anyone who was sharing your MobileMe calendars will immediately lose access to those shared calendars, unless they also migrate to iCloud. For example, my wife and I share many of our calendars, as well as each of us having private calendars. When I began preparing this book, I moved my calendars to iCloud, and immediately she lost access to my calendars, and I to hers. It wasn't until I cajoled her into both upgrading to Mac OS X Lion and migrating to iCloud that we got our calendars back into sync by resubscribing to each other's calendars in iCloud. So I recommend that if you share your calendars with one or more people, that you all be prepared to make the move to iCloud at virtually the same time, to avoid disruption.

set to trigger on your iOS device when the device is physically near a location, using your device's GPS and Location Services. Even cooler, geofencing can be set to trigger the reminder when you arrive at or leave a particular location. So that's how the Siri personal assistant built into the iPhone 4S and later can deal with commands like "Text my wife when I leave the office."

In this book, I'm focusing on iCloud, rather than working with iCal or the iOS Calendar app, so I'll deal mostly with working with events on the iCloud website, rather than in the Mac or iOS programs. However, because Reminders are so intimately connected with iCloud, I'll be going into detail with the iOS Reminders app in the "Working with Reminders on Your iOS Device" section, later in this chapter.

To create a calendar on a Mac:

1. Launch iCal .

2. Choose File > New Calendar > then either iCloud or On My Mac C.

   Choosing iCloud will place the calendar on iCloud, where it can be shared by your other devices and by other people. If the calendar is on your Mac, it will be private and will only exist on the Mac where you created the calendar.

3. The Calendars popover appears, allowing you to name the new calendar **D**. Enter the name, then click anywhere else to save it.

B On the Mac, iCal for Mac OS X Lion has a faux-leather look that people either love or hate.

C Choose where you want to create your new calendar.

D Name the new calendar in the Calendars popover.

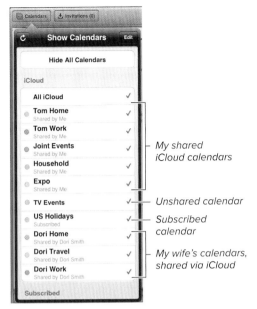

My shared
iCloud calendars

Unshared calendar

Subscribed
calendar

My wife's calendars,
shared via iCloud

E On the iPad, the Show Calendars popover tells you the status of all your iCloud calendars.

F Type the name you want for your new calendar.

To create a calendar on an iOS device:

1. On your iPhone or iPad, start the Calendar app.

2. Tap the Calendars button.

   The Calendars (iPhone) or Show Calendars (iPad) popover appears **E**.

3. Tap the Edit button.

   The screen name changes to Edit Calendars.

4. At the bottom of the iCloud section, tap Add Calendar.

5. In the resulting Add Calendar popover **F**, delete the name *Untitled Calendar*, then type the name you want for the new calendar.

6. Tap next to the color you want the calendar events to appear as.

   You may be able to see additional colors by scrolling.

7. Tap Done.

   The popover will go back to the Edit Calendars screen, and the new calendar you created appears in the list.

8. Tap Done.

To edit a calendar on a Mac:

1. In iCal, click the Calendars button at the upper left corner of the window.

   The Calendars popover appears.

2. Right-click the calendar you want to change, and choose Get Info.

   The info dialog appears for that calendar .

3. Do one or more of the following:

   ▸ Change the name of the calendar.

   ▸ From the color pop-up menu next to the Name field, choose the color in which you want the calendar's events to appear. One difference in iCal versus the Calendar app on iOS is that one of the color choices is Other, which when chosen brings up a color picker that allows you to choose any color you want, rather than a preset color.

4. Click OK.

G In iCal on the Mac, each calendar has an info dialog.

To edit a calendar on an iOS device:

1. On your iPhone or iPad, start the Calendar app.

2. Tap the Calendars button.

   The Calendars (iPhone) or Show Calendars (iPad) popover appears Ⓓ.

3. Tap the Edit button.

   The screen name changes to Edit Calendars.

4. In the Calendar list, tap the name of an existing calendar.

5. In the Edit Calendar screen, change the name or the associated color of the calendar, then tap Done.

Using Alternative Calendar Programs with iCloud

Just because iCal comes with Mac OS X, that doesn't mean that it's universally beloved, or even especially liked, by people who are heavy calendar users. For those people (like me) who have been using calendars on a computer for a very long time, and have used excellent calendar programs over the years, iCal is too limited, too lowest-common-denominator, for our comfort. The trouble is that all of the really useful calendar features (event synchronization between devices, calendar sharing between people) use iCal (or at least its data file) and iCloud as a conduit.

Happily, if iCal isn't feature-rich enough for your needs, a variety of alternative calendar programs still use the iCal calendar and reminders data and provide a superior calendaring experience. My favorite for Mac is BusyMac's BusyCal **H**, which allows you to share events and to-dos over iCloud, MobileMe, or Google Calendar; gives you much more flexibility in calendar views; has easier event entry than iCal; has a wide variety of event types, such as all-day banners, sticky notes in the calendar, and graphics; and much more (BusyCal is also compatible with iCloud calendars even when it is running on a Mac with Mac OS X 10.6 Snow Leopard, making calendar sharing possible for people who haven't yet upgraded to Lion). Another good iCal alternative for the Mac is Flexibits' Fantastical, which lives in your menubar and drops down when you need it. One really attractive thing about Fantastical is that it understands natural-language requests, so you can simply enter "Lunch next Tuesday at 2 with Cliff" and the program correctly parses the sentence and sets the calendar event.

On iOS, there are many alternatives for the Calendar app, but the one I use is called Calvetica **I**, from Mysterious Trousers. I like it because of its minimalist design, and because it requires just a couple of taps (and the text entry for the event name, of course) to enter an event, far fewer than Calendar. It's fast, lets you create an event quickly, and gets out of your way.

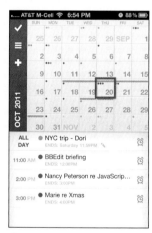

H I prefer to use BusyCal over iCal, because it shows me more information at a glance, such as the mini-months, the reminders list, and the detail for the selected event.

I On iOS, the faster you can enter an event the better, which is why I prefer Calvetica, rather than the stock Calendars app.

Working with Calendars on the iCloud Website

The iCloud website gives you a great deal of control over your calendar and reminders. With it, you can add, view, and change events and reminders; manage calendars and reminders lists; and share your calendars with others (for that last, see the "Sharing Your Calendars with Others" section, later in this chapter).

In this section, all the action will take place on the iCloud website. We'll begin by creating, editing, and deleting calendars, then move on to working with calendar events.

To create a calendar:

1. Go to the iCloud website, and login using your iCloud Apple ID and password.

2. On the iCloud Home screen **Ⓐ**, click Calendar.

   The Calendar screen appears **Ⓑ**.

Ⓐ On the iCloud website, click the Calendar icon to get started.

Show/Hide Calendars List *Calendar View buttons* *Notifications* *Actions pop-up menu*

Go to Today *Year and Month selector* *New Event*

Ⓑ You can do almost anything that you can do in iCal on the iCloud website.

C Choose New Calendar from the Actions pop-up menu.

D Type the name of your new calendar.

3. Click the Actions button at the upper-right of the window.

   The Actions pop-up menu appears C.

4. Choose New Calendar.

   A new calendar appears at the bottom of the Calendars List, ready for you to add a name D.

5. Enter the name, then click outside the name field to save it.

   See "Working With Events" later in this chapter to add and edit calendar events.

To view (or not) a calendar or the Calendars List:

In the Calendars List, select the checkbox next to a calendar's name to see that's calendar's contents. If the checkbox is cleared, the events associated with that calendar will disappear from your calendar views. Nothing's happened to the events; you are simply choosing not to see them.

or

If you want to hide the Calendars List, click the Show/Hide Calendars List button at the top of the window. Clicking the button again will bring the list back.

E To enter calendar Edit mode, click the Edit link.

F In Edit mode, you can change the calendar color, its name, or delete the calendar.

G Clicking the color button brings up a color picker.

H Make sure you really want to delete that calendar!

To edit or delete a calendar:

1. In the iCloud website's Calendar screen, click the Edit link at the top of the Calendars list at the upper-left corner of the window **E**.

   The Calendars list changes into edit mode **F**.

2. Do one or more of the following:

   ▸ To change the color associated with the calendar, click the color button next to the name of the calendar, then choose a different color from the popover **G**. You can also click the Custom color link to pop up a more full-featured color picker, if you don't like the six standard choices.

   ▸ Click in the name field of the calendar, and change it to rename the calendar.

   ▸ To delete a calendar, click the red button with a minus sign in it. As usual when you're potentially about to destroy data, iCloud warns you and asks if you're sure **H**. If you are, click Delete Calendar.

3. When you're done changing your calendars, Click the Done link.

TIP That dialog isn't joking; remember that iCloud is the master repository for all your data. So if you delete that calendar, it and all of its events will disappear not just from the iCloud website but from all your Macs and iOS devices as well. Be careful!

TIP Note that a Plus button also appears when you're editing calendars **F**. Yes, that means that it's another way to add a calendar.

To change calendar views:

On the iCloud website, you have a choice of Day, Week, Month, or List calendar views. Click one of the Calendar View buttons in the toolbar Ⓑ to view the calendar as you wish.

To change date views:

At the bottom of the window, you'll find the Date selector Ⓘ. This selector changes depending on the calendar view. For example, if the Month view is set, you'll see years and months in the Date selector. If the Day or List view is set, you'll see individual days in the selector. Do one or more of the following (assuming the Month view is active; the other views are similar in operation):

- Click one of the months to view its contents.

Previous year   *Months in current year*   *Next year*

Previous *Current year*   *Next*

Ⓘ The Date selector changes, depending on the calendar view.

Go to Date: 8/7/2012

◀ August 2012 ▶

Sun	Mon	Tue	Wed	Thu	Fri	Sat
			1	2	3	4
5	6	7	8	9	10	11
12	13	14	15	16	17	18
19	20	21	22	23	24	25
26	27	28	29	30	31	

Cancel   OK

J You can jump to dates many months or years away with this date picker.

- Click the Previous or Next buttons to move to the previous or next month. If you're already viewing January or December, your view will change to the previous or next year.

- Click the Previous Year or Next Year buttons to change the calendar view by an entire year.

- Click the Today button at the lower left corner of the window to jump to today's date.

- If you need to view a date that's more than a few clicks away, click the Actions menu **C** and choose Go to Date. The resulting date picker **J** allows you to type or navigate to the date you want. Choose that date, then click OK.

Working with Events

The Calendar application on the iCloud website makes it easy to create or change events. Its abilities are very similar to iCal or the iOS Calendar app, but there are a couple of differences. With the website, you can't mark an event as one that shows that you are Busy or Free.

To create an event:

1. In the Calendars List, click to select the calendar in which you want to create the event.

2. Do one or more of the following, and the New Event popover appears:

   ▸ In Month view, double-click in the day in which you want the event.

   ▸ In Day, Week, or List view, drag the mouse cursor across a time range to create an event that covers that range.

   ▸ In any view, click the New Event button (it looks like a plus) in the lower-right corner of the window. When you do this, the event is created on the date you last selected in the calendar.

   ▸ From the Actions pop-up menu, choose New Event.

K Get to know the New Event popover well, because you'll be seeing it a lot.

https://www.icloud.com

"David and Care's Party" will start today at 9:39 PM.

OK

L One of the places that alerts can appear is on the iCloud website.

3. In the New Event popover **K**, do one or more of the following:

▸ Enter the title of the event.

▸ (Optional) Enter the event's location.

▸ (Optional) If the event is going to last all day, click the all-day checkbox.

▸ In the From section, set the event's starting date and time.

▸ In the To section, set the event's ending date and time.

▸ (Optional) If this will be a recurring event, choose the recurring schedule from the pop-up menu next to Repeat. You can choose Every Day, Every Week, Every Month, Every Year, or Custom. If you choose Custom, you get a pop-up dialog that allows you to choose dates with any flexibility you want on a Daily, Weekly, Monthly, or Yearly basis. The Monthly or Yearly Custom choices also allow you to choose intervals such as the first, second, third, fourth, or last days of a month.

▸ (Optional) If you want to be reminded before the event starts, choose from the Alert pop-up menu, and select the interval before the event. If you set an alert, a 2nd Alert pop-up menu appears, allowing you to set an interval for a second reminder. Alerts appear as notifications on your iOS devices, and also in iCal on your Mac, and as a dialog on the iCloud website in your browser **L**.

continues on next page

- ▸ (Optional) If you want, you can change the calendar for the event with a pop-up menu in the Calendar section.

- ▸ (Optional) If you want to invite friends or colleagues to the event, enter their name or email address into the Invitees field. As you type, iCloud looks up a matching contact in your iCloud contacts list, providing a pop-up menu with possible matches. Select a contact from the menu to accept it. You can add multiple invitees to an event. If your invitees use iCloud, the invitation will appear in the Notifications button on the iCloud website, in iCal, and in the Calendar app on their iOS devices. Invitees have the option to Accept, Decline, or mark the event as Maybe.

- ▸ (Optional) You can also add a note to the event, perhaps with details about the meeting.

4. Click OK to save the event.

   The event appears on your calendar.

To edit an event:

Double-click an event in your calendar to bring up the popover with the event details, change the details you desire, then click OK.

or

In the Date or Week views, drag the top or bottom border of an event on the calendar to change its duration.

To move an event:

Do one or more of the following:

- On the calendar, drag the event from one location to where you want it. For example, you might want to move the meeting that is been rescheduled from one day to the next.

- Double-click the event to open its pop-up window, then change the event details. You might need to use both these techniques if an event is moved both in day and time.

To delete an event:

In any calendar view, click an event to select it, then press the Delete or Backspace keys.

or

Double-click the event to bring up the popover with the event details, then click the Delete button.

TIP If I'm going to be making a lot of changes to my calendar events or reminders, I'll often choose to do them on my Mac, rather than on an iOS device, because I still find it easier to use a separate hardware keyboard and mouse, rather than tapping and swiping on a touch-screen. Perhaps I'm a dinosaur.

Sharing Your Calendars with Others

Perhaps the most useful thing about iCloud's calendar is its ability to share your calendars and events with family, colleagues, and friends who are also using iCloud. You can allow other people to share any of your calendars, and they can ask you to share theirs. Of course, you can still have calendars that are private to you; iCloud will synchronize those private calendars among all your devices, but nobody else will be able to see them. You can have any mix of shared and private calendars you want.

There's a difference between *sharing* and *inviting*. When you share, you're sharing a whole calendar and *all* its events with another iCloud user. When you invite, you are offering to share a particular event with another person, whether or not they are using iCloud. Keep this difference in mind when you decide which of the kinds of collaboration you want. For example, I'm comfortable in sharing most of my calendars with my wife. But there might be a particular meeting on my Work calendar that I have with an editor; rather than share the whole calendar, I'd be likely to simply invite that editor to only that one meeting; the invitation will be sent via email. When the editor accepts the invitation, the event appears for both of us.

iCloud's calendar sharing uses the industry-standard CalDAV protocol, so you can share calendars with people running iCal or variety of other calendar programs on the Mac, and Microsoft Outlook 2007 or later on Windows.

Private calendars

Shared calendars

A The icons next to the calendars tell you the calendar's sharing status.

B Enter the name and the sharing privileges for each person with which you want to share the calendar.

To turn on calendar sharing:

1. On the calendar application of the iCloud website, the Calendars List will show a Share icon next to each calendar **A**. A gray icon indicates the calendar isn't being shared, and a green icon indicates that it is.

2. Click a gray icon to begin the sharing process.

   The Share Calendar popover appears **B**.

3. In most cases, you're going to want to share the calendar privately with one or more people. Click the Private Calendar radio button, then in the field underneath, begin typing the person's name or email address. iCloud will do a lookup of your Contacts list and provide a pop-up menu with possible matches. Click a contact with the mouse to select it.

4. Choose whether you want the person to be able to View & Edit the calendar (that's the default choice) or to just be able to View the calendar.

   You might want to make a calendar read-only (the View choice) if the events of the calendar are ones that you merely want to have the other person informed about, but not to be able to change, such as your business travel plans.

continues on next page

5. (Optional) Repeat steps 3 and 4 for anyone else you want to share the calendar with.

6. Click Share.

iCloud displays a confirmation message , and sends email invitations to the people you chose . If they accept the invitation by clicking the Join Calendar button in the email, they'll be added to the calendar.

7. (Optional) If you click the Email me when this calendar is changed checkbox, you'll get an email when anyone other than you makes a change to the calendar.

8. Click OK.

TIP If you share one of your calendars, you are considered to be the calendar's owner. Only you have the right to allow other people to view or edit the calendar. Conversely, if you are sharing someone else's calendar you only have the privileges they have allowed you. And you can't change those privileges for yourself or anyone else.

TIP To check the status of a calendar you don't own, click the green Share icon next to it. iCloud will show you the Shared Calendar Info popover .

TIP To remove someone from calendar sharing of the calendar you own, click the Share icon, which brings up the Share Calendar popover. The popover will show you the people who are currently sharing the calendar. Click on the person who you would like to remove from sharing, then click the red minus icon next to their name.

TIP You can stop sharing a calendar altogether by clicking the Share icon, which brings up the Share Calendar popover, and clicking the Stop Sharing button at the bottom. You'll get the usual iCloud confirmation dialog; click Stop Sharing again.

C When the sharing process is underway, iCloud lets you know.

D Invitees get an email invitation to your calendars. Accepting the invitation is as easy as clicking the Join Calendar button.

E You can see who is sharing calendars that you don't own.

A Apple maintains a list of public calendars.

Subscribing to Public Calendars

Besides the calendar events of yourself, family, friends, and colleagues, you might be interested in importing other kinds of calendars. For example, you might want to subscribe to an automatically updated calendar for holidays in your country. Or if you're a sports fan, you might want the playing schedule for your favorite team to appear in your calendar. Maybe you want the local weather, or the phases of the moon. All of these, and many more, are available as public calendars to which you can subscribe. You'll typically use iCal on the Mac to subscribe to one of these calendars, but once you do, you can choose to either keep that calendar local to your Mac, or to share it with the rest of your devices via iCloud.

In this section, I'm going to show you how to find a public calendar using iCal, subscribe to it, and then view it in your calendar.

To subscribe to a public calendar:

1. Open iCal on your Mac.

2. Choose Calendar > Find Subscriptions.

   Your default web browser will open and bring you to Apple's list of available public iCal calendars Ⓐ. at the top of the list, you can choose to view the calendar feeds by Most recent, Most popular, or Alphabetical.

3. Find the calendar to which you wish to subscribe, then click the Download button for that calendar.

   Depending on the source of the calendar, you may be taken to a different website where you can choose from a

continues on next page

number of calendars. If so, find the calendar feed you want from that website, then click to subscribe to it.

When you subscribe to a public calendar, iCal shows you a dialog with the URL of the calendar 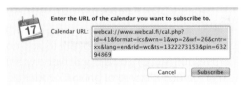.

4. Click Subscribe.

iCal shows you a detail screen about the calendar .

5. Do one or more of the following:

▸ Change the name of the calendar.

▸ From the color pop-up menu next to the Name field, choose the color in which you want the calendar's events to appear.

▸ Using the Location pop-up menu, choose either iCloud or On My Mac. This is probably your most important choice in this dialog; choosing iCloud will make the subscribed calendar appear on all your devices.

▸ By default, most subscribed calendars have Alerts, Attachments, and Reminders removed. In most cases, I recommend you keep it that way.

▸ From the Auto-refresh pop-up menu, choose how often you want the calendar to refresh its data from the original URL.

6. Click OK.

The subscribed calendar appears in iCal. Double-click one of the calendar events to see its details .

TIP You can find public calendars in many more places than just Apple's directory. For example, in the U.S., all the Major League Baseball clubs offer calendars that you can download into iCal.

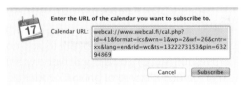
B When you subscribe to a calendar in iCal, it shows you the calendar's URL.

C Subscribing to the calendar gives you its information, and allows you to choose whether you want to subscribe to it only on your local Mac, or via iCloud.

D You can't change the details of the events in a subscribed calendar, but you can view them.

E Right-click the calendar you want to delete, then choose Delete from the shortcut menu.

To delete a subscribed calendar:

1. In iCal, click the Calendars button in the upper left corner of the window.

2. The calendar you want to delete will appear in the Subscriptions section of the calendar list. Right-click that calendar, then choose Delete from the shortcut menu **E**.

   iCal asks you if you're sure you want to delete the calendar.

3. Click Delete.

   The calendar and its events and reminders are deleted. If you had the calendar shared on iCloud, the events and reminders will disappear from all your devices.

Setting iCloud Calendar Preferences

The iCloud Calendar application has two preference panes, General and Advanced. They closely mirror the preferences in iCal.

To set General preferences:

1. Click the Actions button, then choose Preferences from the pop-up menu.

   The General preferences appear **A**.

2. Choose one or more the following:

   ▸ In the Appearance section, choose whether you want to display 5 or 7 days per week, on which day of the week you want the displayed week to start, and how many hours at a time you want to display in the Day and Week views. If you select the Show Birthdays calendar checkbox, the Calendar application will show a new Birthdays calendar, with information taken from the Birthday field of the people in your iCloud Contacts list.

   ▸ In the Format section, choose the Date format (your choices are MM/DD/YYYY, DD/MM/YYYY, and YYYY/MM/DD) and the Time format (12 hour or 24 hour). You can also choose the Date Separator (/, -, or .) and the Time Separator (: or .).

   ▸ In the Alerts section, if you select Add a default alert to new events and invitations, you can choose from the pop-up menu the amount of time before which the event is sched-uled that you'll get an alert on your iCloud-enabled devices. If you select Show alerts in iCloud Calendar, alerts will appear as pop-up dialogs on the iCloud website.

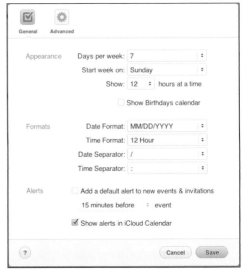

A The General Preferences screen lets you set the calendar's appearance, formats, and alerts.

Time Zone | Enable time zone support
To change your time zone, tap the iCloud button in the toolbar to see the application switcher. Tap on your name and choose View Account.

Old Events & Reminders | ☐ Hide reminders with due dates after the calendar view
☐ Hide reminders ___ days after they've been completed
☐ Hide events ___ days after they've passed

Invitations & Updates | ☑ Ask before sending changes to events
☐ Send me a copy of event invitations and updates
☑ Use iCloud for incoming invitations
Get notifications in Calendar and iCal for invitations from other iCloud users.

? | Cancel | Save

B The Advanced Preferences screen is a potpourri of settings.

To set Advanced preferences:

1. Click the Actions button, then choose Preferences from the pop-up menu.

2. Click the Advanced button in the toolbar.

   The Advanced preferences appear **B**.

3. Choose one or more the following:

   ▸ In the Time Zone section, if you select Enable time zone support, you can change the time zone for the whole calendar, or just for individual events that are different from the time zone you're in. If you choose this, a new Time Zone pop-up menu will appear in the New Event and Edit Event popovers. Choosing a new time zone from the pop-up menu will make Calendar automatically change the time of the event as shown on your calendar to match the chosen time zone. For example, if you're on the West Coast of the United States, you have time zone support enabled, and you set an event to occur at 3 p.m. Eastern time, the event will automatically be translated to noon Pacific time.

   ▸ In the Old Events & Reminders section, select the various checkboxes to hide reminders and events.

   ▸ In the Invitations & Updates section, if you select Ask before sending changes to events (it's on by default), iCloud will check with you before it sends out emails alerting people to changes in events. This keeps changes in your calendar from cluttering other people's mailboxes. Choosing Send me a copy of event invitations and updates is self-explanatory, as is Use iCloud for incoming invitations.

Adding Reminders

The iCloud Calendar application doesn't just deal with calendars and events. It can also work with to-do items, which it refers to as *reminders*. In a major change from the way reminders were handled in MobileMe, reminders in iCloud appear on their own separate calendars, which iCloud calls *reminder lists* 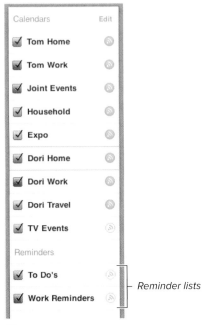. On the iCloud website, reminder lists appear in the Reminders section directly below your Calendar list. On iOS devices, you deal with calendar events and reminders in two entirely separate apps, the Calendar and Reminders apps, respectively . On the Mac, you work with both events and reminders in iCal or other calendar programs that work with iCloud, and on Windows you can use Microsoft Outlook 2007 or later (which calls reminders *Tasks*).

Reminders are different from calendar events, in that they can be checked off as completed; you can assign a priority to them; and you can give them a due date (but you don't have to). Reminders with due dates not yet marked as completed automatically remain in your Reminders list (you can change this behavior somewhat in the Advanced section of Preferences; see the "To set Advanced preferences" section, earlier in this chapter).

In this section, you'll learn how to use the iCloud website to work with reminder lists and reminders. Remember that as you use the iCloud website, changes you make there will automatically propagate to the rest of your iCloud-enabled devices.

Reminder lists

A The Reminder lists appear the bottom of the calendar list.

B On iOS, you use two separate applications to handle events and reminders.

C If it isn't already visible, choose Show Reminders from the Actions pop-up menu to display the Reminders pane.

D The Reminders pane allows you to check off completed tasks, shows you if a task has a priority associated with it, and tells you if a task is overdue.

E Type the name of your new reminder list.

To add a Reminder List on the iCloud website:

1. In your web browser, open the Calendar application on the iCloud website.

2. If the Reminders pane isn't visible, click the Actions button and choose Show Reminders from the pop-up menu **C**.

   The Reminders pane appears on the right side of the window **D**.

3. Click the Actions button and choose New Reminder List from the pop-up menu **C**.

   In the Reminders section below your Calendars list, a new reminder list appears, ready for you to name it **E**.

4. Enter a name for the list, then click anywhere in the Calendar view to save the new name.

TIP You can change the color assigned to the reminder list and its name, you can share it, and you can delete it, just as you would any other calendar. See the corresponding sections for doing those actions with calendars, earlier in this chapter, to see how.

To add Reminders on the iCloud website:

1. In your web browser, open the Calendar application on the iCloud website.

2. If the Reminders pane isn't visible, click the Actions button and choose Show Reminders from the pop-up menu.

3. Select one of the reminder lists and choose Actions > New Reminder.

   or

   Double-click in an empty area of the Reminders pane.

   The New Reminder popover appears **F**.

4. Do one or more of the following:

   ▶ Enter the reminder title.

   ▶ From the Priority pop-up menu, assign the reminder's priority level (None, Low, Medium, or High). If you assign a priority, the reminder will show the priority as an icon of one or more exclamation points in the Reminders pane, as shown in the Priority pop-up menu **G**.

   ▶ If you want to assign a Due Date to the reminder, select that checkbox, then enter a date in the field that appears. Interestingly, the iCloud website doesn't allow you to also add a time, whereas the Reminders iOS app does.

F The New Reminder popover is how you'll be adding your tasks.

G You can choose a priority for a reminder.

- ▸ (Optional) If you assigned a due date, the Alert pop-up menu appears. If you want an alert, pick one of the choices from the pop-up menu (None, 1 day before, 2 days before, or On date of reminder).
- ▸ If you like, you can change the Reminder List for the reminder.
- ▸ If you want, add a Note to the reminder.

5. Click OK.

   The new reminder appears in the Reminders pane.

To edit or delete a reminder:

1. Double-click a reminder in the Reminders pane.

   A popover appears with the reminder's details.

2. Change the aspects of the reminder you wish, then click OK.

   or

   To delete the reminder, click the Delete button in the popover.

TIP A faster way to delete a reminder is to select it in the **Reminders pane**, then press **Delete or Backspace.**

TIP You can mark a reminder as completed by clicking the checkbox next to it in the Reminders pane.

TIP Clicking the Reminders header at the top of the reminders pane allows you to sort your reminders by due date, priority, title, or list.

Working with Reminders on Your iOS Device

As mentioned before, you work with iCloud reminders on an iOS device in the Reminders app, which was introduced with iOS 5. Even though a reminders list is a kind of calendar, it makes sense to me that Apple chose to separate managing events and reminders on mobile devices, because adding the interface necessary to properly deal with reminders into the Calendar iOS app would have made the app feel as though those reminder features were shoehorned in.

In this section, you'll see how to use the Reminders app to set up a to-do. Adding or editing a task in Reminders makes it automatically synchronize with the rest of your iCloud-enabled devices.

Reminders Versus the World

Reminders is a free app from Apple that enters an already very crowded field of iOS task managers, many of which also have Mac application counterparts that they sync with. Examples of apps with Mac versions include The Omni Group's OmniFocus, Appigo's ToDo, and Cultured Code's Things. Task managers that shine on iOS include BusyMac's Busy ToDo (which works with their BusyCal desktop program); Toodledo, from the company of the same name; SmartPad, from Left Coast Logic; and WebIS' Pocket Informant. Reminders also competes with iOS apps that are front ends to Web-based task management services, such as Remember the Milk's eponymous app.

So how does Reminders stack up in this crowd? Well, it's kind of the same situation as with calendaring. The Apple app does the job, but has a set of features that will leave power users wanting more, *more*, MORE! Reminders, based as it is around a calendar metaphor, doesn't have important features for hardcore task management warriors, such as the concept of grouping tasks into projects, or the ability to organize a bunch of tasks and show you the most important next action that needs doing. For devotees of the Getting Things Done or Franklin Covey organization methods, Reminders is not going to cut the mustard.

But let's say that you don't have such a complicated life, you don't care about organizing tasks into projects, and you just want a decent to-do list. My advice is that you start with Reminders. If you find yourself after a while wanting more organizational control, there are plenty of apps in the App Store that can scratch that itch, starting with the ones I've listed above.

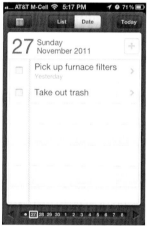

A You'll work with your tasks in the Reminders app. This is the List view.

B You can see tasks with associated due date in the Date view.

C The Reminders app on the iPad gives you a nice set of mini-months, making it easier to jump to future dates.

To set a reminder:

1. Start the Reminders app.

   The app appears, set to its default List view **A**. To see your tasks that have due dates, tap the Date button **B**. Note that tasks that don't have due dates will not appear in the Date view, though all tasks assigned to a particular list (whether they have dates or not) will show when you select that list in List view.

   On the iPhone or iPod touch, you can move between your different reminders lists in List view by swiping right or left. Similarly, in Date view, you can change the date by swiping right or left, or by tapping a date in the navigation bar at the bottom of the screen. On the iPad, with its larger screen, you can see more information at one time **C**.

2. In either List or Date view, tap the plus button to add a reminder.

   In the list that you're on, on the first blank line, an insertion point appears.

continues on next page

3. Type the reminder title

4. (Optional) You can tap the Return key and enter more tasks.

5. On an iPhone or iPod touch, tap the Done button. On an iPad, tap somewhere other than the line you're typing in, or tap the Hide Keyboard key 🔽.

   The new reminder appears in the list.

6. To adjust the reminder's details, tap it in the list. A Details screen or popover (on the iPad) appears ⓔ.

   On this screen, you can set a time or geographical reminder by tapping Remind Me.

   or

   If you tap Show More, you have the opportunity to set the reminder's Priority, change its assigned reminders list, or add Notes.

8. To set a due date or geographical reminder, tap Remind Me.

ⓓ Enter the title for your reminder.

ⓔ On the Details screen, you can choose to set a reminder date or location, or you can add other information to the reminder.

F You can set either time or location-based reminders.

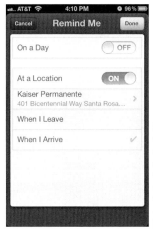

G If you choose to be reminded at a location, you can also choose whether that reminder triggers when you leave or arrive at the location.

9. On the resulting Remind Me screen **F**, you can turn on either (or both) On a Day and At a Location.

   If you choose On a Day, Reminders will show you the standard date and time picker. Choose when you want to be reminded, then tap Done.

   If you choose At a Location, the Location screen will appear, showing your current location, your Home and Work locations from your iCloud Contacts list, and a Choose Address button. Tapping that button opens your Contacts list, from which you can choose the location where you want to be reminded. Pick a contact with an address, and you'll be returned to the Location screen. When you tap the Remind Me button, you'll see the contact name and address **G**. You'll also get two new options, When I Leave and When I Arrive. Choose one of these.

10. Tap Done.

TIP Location-based reminders are associated with the iPhone 4 and 4S. They don't work on earlier iPhones, the iPad, or iPod touch. Reminders with location information still appear on those other devices, but the location-specific information doesn't appear. As I write this, it's unclear if this is a bug that will be fixed or not.

Reminders or Alarms?

With the advent of the Reminders iOS app, you now have more than one way to alert yourself when things need doing. You can use the Reminders app, as described above. But for some purposes, you might want to instead use the Alarm function of the iPhone's Clock app. Let's take a look at the differences between the two approaches.

The Reminders app is associated with your iCloud calendars and to-dos, and as a result synchronizes across all of your devices. That's great when you want that to happen, but sometimes you don't. For example, let's say that you need to take a medication each evening. You could certainly set up a Reminder for that, and it would appear on your Reminder List every day. That would tend to clutter up the Reminder List, especially if you had similar routine reminders. When the Reminder triggers, because it is associated with iCloud and synchronizes between your devices, you'll get alerts on all your devices, and you'll need to dismiss those alerts on all devices. I've certainly found it to be jarring when I had my iPhone, iPad, and Mac all in one room, and they all popped up a Reminder alert and made a noise at the same time.

On the other hand, the Clock app only runs on the iPhone, which you often carry on your person, and you can set it up to give you a recurring alarm (as well as setting as many different alarms you need in a particular day). Because it's not integrated with iCloud, there is no calendar clutter. And the Clock app's repeating function ⒽⒽ has day-of-the-week options that the Reminders app does not ⒾⒾ. By the way, if you need multiple reminders in the same day, there's a terrific app called HabiTimer from Sciral that's perfect for things that neither Clock nor Reminders does well, like alerting you to take medications multiple times in a day.

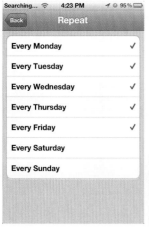

Ⓗ In the Clock app, you have a bit more flexibility in terms of recurring day-of-the-week alarms.

Ⓘ The Reminders app allows you to set reminders at intervals up to a year away.

5

Using iPhoto with iCloud

Photo Stream, part of the iCloud service, solves a familiar problem. You take a photo *here*, but you'd like to view it or work on it over *there*. For example, you might have taken a picture with your iPhone (following the ancient adage that the best camera is the one that you have with you), then want to add it to your iPhoto library on your Mac. Or maybe you imported a bunch of pictures into iPhoto from your digital camera, and you'd like to show them off to people using your iPad. With Photo Stream, your new photos will be uploaded to the iCloud servers and will automagically be pushed to your other iCloud-enabled devices when they are connected to Wi-Fi.

On the Mac, Photo Stream works with Apple's iPhoto or Aperture programs. Since those programs don't exist on Windows, you can designate automatic download and upload folders on your PC's hard disk for use with Photo Stream.

Setting up Photo Stream in iCloud

Photos uploaded to Photo Stream are stored in iCloud for 30 days. Your iOS devices keep a rolling collection of the last 1,000 photos in your Photo Stream, in order to make the best use of their limited storage. Since computers generally have way more storage space than mobile devices, all of the photos that are part of your Photo Stream are kept on your Mac or PC, even if you shoot more than 1,000 photos in a month.

Photo Stream supports JPEG, TIF, PNG, and most RAW photo formats. On a computer, your photos will be downloaded and stored in full resolution. iCloud delivers photos to your iOS device (iPhone, iPad, iPod touch, and Apple TV), in a reduced resolution to save storage space and speed up download times. And while we're on the subject of storage space, pictures in your Photo Stream don't count against the 5 GB of free storage that you get with your iCloud account.

TIP **Photo Stream only works with still photos, not with video.**

TIP **The system requirements for Photo Stream on a Mac are the same as for iCloud in general. On a PC, you'll need to be running Microsoft Windows 7 or Windows Vista with Service Pack 2. You can download the Windows iCloud control panel from `http://support.apple.com/kb/DL1455`. After downloading, double-click the iCloudSetup.exe file to install the control panel.**

To enable Photo Stream on either a Mac or PC, you'll use the iCloud preference pane (Mac) or Control Panel (Windows).

A You enable Photo Stream in the iCloud preference pane on a Mac.

B On a Windows PC, you use the iCloud Control Panel to enable Photo Stream. Note the Options button.

C On Windows, if you want to change the download and upload folders, you can do so in the Photo Stream Options dialog.

To enable Photo Stream on your Mac or PC:

1. On a Mac, choose System Preferences > iCloud **A**.

    or

    On a PC, choose Start Menu > Control Panel > Network and Internet > iCloud **B**.

2. On either platform, select the checkbox next to Photo Stream.

    On the Mac, close the System Preferences window. On Windows, click Apply, then close the iCloud control panel.

3. (Optional) On a PC, you can choose to change the default folders Photo Stream uses for uploads and downloads. Click the Options button **B** to display the Photo Stream Options dialog **C**. The dialog shows you the default paths to the download and upload folders; click the Change buttons next to either of those folders to switch them to a different location on your PC's hard drive, navigate to the new locations, select the location, then click OK. Back in the Options dialog, click OK again.

Setting up Photo Stream on your iOS device:

1. Choose > Settings > iCloud 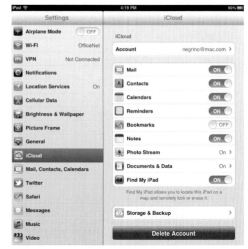.

2. Tap Photo Stream.

   The screen changes to show the Photo Stream preferences **E**.

3. Slide the switch to On.

   If your mobile device is connected to Wi-Fi, it will immediately begin down-loading photos from the iCloud servers, and uploading new photos.

> **TIP** If you want to remove the Photo Stream from your iOS device, simply turn it Off in Settings. The Photo Stream photos will be removed from your iOS device, but will remain on the iCloud servers.

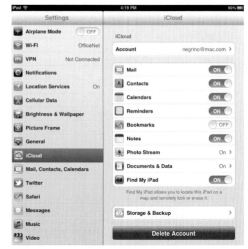

D Begin setting up Photo Stream on an iOS device in the iCloud Settings.

E When you turn the Photo Stream switch to On, photos will automatically begin uploading and downloading.

Photo Stream Drawbacks

The ability of Photo Stream to automatically make your photos appear on all of your devices is quite useful. However, iCloud is missing some functionality compared to the previous photo capa-bilities in MobileMe. For example, as of this writing, you can't view your Photo Stream on the iCloud website. There's no iCloud equivalent yet to the MobileMe Gallery, so you can't share Events or Albums online. And of course, because you can't view your Photo Stream online, you also can't edit or delete individual photos from the Photo Stream from the iCloud website (actually, you can't delete individual photos at all, though there are workarounds as detailed in the "Deleting Photos" section later in this chapter). These features are so obvious that I expect Apple to add them sooner or later, but for now Photo Stream feels a bit unfinished.

A Photo Stream appears as just another source in the iPhoto sidebar.

Working with Photo Stream in iPhoto

Pictures from Photo Stream appear in iPhoto '11 (version 9.2.1 or later) in a new entry in the iPhoto sidebar **A**. Clicking this entry in the sidebar shows you the pictures in your Photo Stream **B**. It's important to understand that pictures that appear in your Photo Stream haven't yet been imported into your photo library; you'll either need to enable Automatic Import or manually import the photos in a separate step, as described later in this section.

Photo Stream works with either iPhoto or Apple's Aperture (see the "The Aperture Alternative" sidebar in this section), but not both at the same time. You have to choose which program you'll use with Photo Stream, and turning the feature on in one program automatically turns it off in the other.

B Clicking Photo Stream in the sidebar displays the photos in the iPhoto document window.

In either program's preferences, you can decide whether or not you want the program to automatically import Photo Stream photos into the program's Events, Photos, Faces, and Places, and, if you want, automatically upload those imported photos to the iCloud servers.

Since automatically pushing your photos to all your devices is the whole point of Photo Stream, why wouldn't you want to automatically upload photos to iCloud? Remember that Photo Stream accepts full resolution photos from digital cameras, so if you're shooting RAW format photos with your digital SLR, then importing them on a computer, iPhoto or Aperture will automatically upload all those pictures, which could potentially be many gigabytes in size. If you happen to live in an area with slow Internet connections or metered data, uploading those pictures could get very expensive (and if your iOS devices are on your Wi-Fi network, you'll also incur bandwidth for downloading the resolution-optimized versions of those photos when they get pushed to your mobile devices). In that case, you might want to deselect the Automatic Upload checkbox in the Photo Stream preferences in your photo management application.

TIP **There's also a caveat in allowing automatic upload to Photo Stream from your iOS device. If you're the kind of person (and you know who you are) who could happen to shoot a potentially embarrassing picture with your iPhone, it will automatically be pushed up to iCloud and down to your iPad and computers. So if you share the latter devices with other people, they'll immediately see the photographic evidence. See "Deleting Photos," later in this chapter, for a possible remedy for your faux pas.**

C Enable Photo Stream in iPhoto's preferences.

D If you turn Photo Stream off, iPhoto warns you that you will lose photos that you have not imported into your iPhoto library.

To set Photo Stream preferences:

1. Choose iPhoto > Preferences > Photo Stream **C**.

   or

   Choose Aperture > Preferences > Photo Stream.

2. Select the Enable Photo Stream checkbox.

   By default, the Automatic Import and Automatic Upload checkboxes are also selected. Deselect one or both, according to your needs.

To disable Photo Stream in your photo program:

1. Open the Photo Stream preferences of your photo program.

2. Deselect the checkbox next to Enable Photo Stream.

   The photo program warns you that all the photos in the Photo Stream view will be removed **D**. You may already have imported all the photos into your photo library, but it's still usually a good idea to click the Import Photos and Turn Off button. It won't duplicate already imported pictures.

To import Photo Stream items into an iPhoto or Aperture library:

1. Click on Photo Stream in the sidebar of your photo management program.

2. Select individual photos in the Photo Stream. You can use the Shift key to select multiple contiguous photos, or use the Command key to select multiple noncontiguous photos.

3. Drag the selected photos to the Photos item in the sidebar .

   If you inadvertently try to import photos that have already been imported, the program will let you know and allow you to decide what you want to do .

E To import photos from your Photo Stream into the iPhoto library, select them in the document window, then drag them to Photos in the sidebar.

F iPhoto helps you deal with accidentally importing duplicate photos.

The Aperture Alternative

Photo Stream doesn't just work in iPhoto; it also works with Apple's Aperture program (version 3.2 or later). Aperture is Apple's high-end photo application; you can think of it as (and Apple positions it as) iPhoto Pro. Compared to iPhoto, Aperture gives you many more tools for retouching, editing, adding effects, and managing your photos. Aperture is designed to work with very large photo libraries, and unlike iPhoto, you can maintain separate Aperture libraries to better segregate your different kinds of photography.

When you enable Photo Stream in Aperture, it appears as just another category in your library **G**. If you try to enable Photo Stream in Aperture and the feature is already turned on in iPhoto, Aperture gives you the opportunity to switch the Photo Stream **H**, which automatically turns off the feature in iPhoto.

G Like iPhoto, Aperture displays Photo Stream as another choice in its Library.

H If you already have iPhoto selected as the destination for your Photo Stream and you try to turn it on in Aperture, the program lets you know it will be switching the Photo Stream to Aperture from iPhoto.

Deleting Photos

Control of Photo Stream on iCloud isn't very granular. You can't view the Photo Stream on the iCloud website, and you can't delete individual pictures from the Photo Stream. What you can do is reset your entire Photo Stream, deleting from the server or from individual devices.

To delete your Photo Stream photos from the iCloud server, you'll use the iCloud website. To delete Photo Stream photos from your photo management program or your iOS devices, you simply turn off Photo Stream in the Preferences of the program or the iCloud Settings of the device. On a PC, you need to delete any photos in the Import folder.

If you want to completely delete all of the photos in your Photo Stream, you'll need to first reset your Photo Stream on the iCloud website, then turn Photo Stream off from your various devices.

> **TIP** If you leave Photo Stream enabled on any of your devices, that device will refill iCloud with all of the photos you deleted from the website (at least the last 1,000 photos that were pushed to the mobile device).

To delete your Photo Stream on the iCloud website:

1. Log in to the iCloud website.
2. Click your name on the iCloud homepage.
3. Click the Advanced button.
4. In the Advanced screen , click the Reset Photo Stream button.

   A confirmation dialog will appear .
5. Click Reset.

   The photos will immediately be deleted from your Photo Stream.

Ⓐ You can delete your Photo Stream photos from the iCloud servers on the iCloud website.

Ⓑ As usual when you want to do something destructive, you'll get a confirmation dialog.

> **TIP** If you had Automatic Import enabled in your Photo Stream settings in iPhoto or Aperture, your Photo Stream photos were imported into your program's library, and will remain after you disable Photo Stream. You can, of course, manually delete any of these photos in the programs.

> **TIP** If you turn Photo Stream off on your iOS device, you'll lose access to the Photo Stream on that device, and it will also stop uploading new pictures to the Photo Stream. If you turn Photo Stream back on, any new photos you shoot will start flowing to iCloud again, but any photos you took while Photo Stream was off won't be uploaded.

6

Using iTunes with iCloud

Since the whole point of iCloud is that all your stuff should be on all your devices, it wouldn't make much sense if the contents of your iTunes Library didn't make it to the iCloud party. Happily, almost any music you have in one place can now appear anywhere you want.

Using a feature called iTunes in the Cloud, you can share your purchased iTunes items with up to ten of your (and perhaps your family's) iOS devices and computers. New items you purchase from the iTunes Store automatically appear on all your devices; there's no more need for manual syncing.

You can also purchase a subscription to a service called iTunes Match, which scans your iTunes Library for music tracks you didn't purchase from the iTunes Store. Matched files are replaced by streaming versions from the Store, at full quality. Any tracks that can't be matched are uploaded from your computer to iCloud and can be downloaded to all your devices.

In This Chapter

Configuring iTunes in the Cloud

With its iTunes in the Cloud feature, iCloud has the ability to automatically download purchases to your iOS devices, and re-download purchases that you bought in the past but aren't currently on a particular device.

First, let's talk about automatic downloading. Before iCloud, if you purchased something from the iTunes Store (apps, books, music, movies, or TV shows) you needed to use iTunes to make sure those items were on all of the devices you wanted them on. With iCloud, you can choose to push apps, books, and music automatically to all your devices, no matter on which device you buy the media, as long as you bought the item on the iTunes Store. You can choose to use just Wi-Fi for this automatic downloading, or you can also enable the ability via cellular data. The best part of all this automatic downloading is that it really is automatic: once you set it up, purchased items simply appear on all your devices without you having to worry about item management. Automatic downloading isn't available if you buy music from other online stores, say, Amazon; see the "Configuring and Using iTunes Match" section later in this chapter for a workaround.

TIP Although you can buy TV shows and movies from the iTunes Store, they can't be automatically downloaded, no doubt because they would require so much bandwidth. You can, however, copy video to your iOS device via Wi-Fi, not just USB; that's one of the new features of iOS 5.

A Turn on automatic downloads in iTunes' Preferences.

You also have the ability to re-download items to your iOS device. Imagine that you had previously purchased something from the iTunes Store, and you removed it from your iOS device to free up some space. Or perhaps there was an app that you previously used only on your iPhone, but now you would also like it on your iPad. Or if you replace an iOS device with a newer model, you can choose which purchased items you would like to put on the new device.

To set up automatic downloads on a Mac or PC:

1. In iTunes, choose iTunes > Preferences > Store **A**.

2. In the Automatic Downloads section of the Store dialog, choose one or more of Music, Apps, or Books.

TIP As you would expect, iTunes does the right thing when it comes to the appropriateness of its automatic downloading. For example, an app that works only on an iPad won't be downloaded to an iPhone or iPod touch.

To set up automatic downloads on iOS:

1. On your iOS device, tap Settings > Store.

2. On the Store screen **B**, choose which items (Music, Apps, or Books) you want to automatically download.

3. (Optional) Turn on Use Cellular Data. On devices with 3G support, this will use the cellular data network to download your purchases, not just Wi-Fi.

B On an iOS device, you turn on automatic downloads in the Store section of Settings.

TIP The drawback of using cellular data for automatic downloads is that you may go over your cellular data limitation (in countries and with cellular carriers that impose such caps).

TIP For publications that appear in iOS 5's Newsstand app, you can turn automatic downloading on or off for each publication you have installed in Newsstand. Because each publication is actually a different app (even though it shows up in Newsstand, which you can really think of as a specialized folder), you'll find the publication's download settings in the long list of app settings at the bottom of the Setings app.

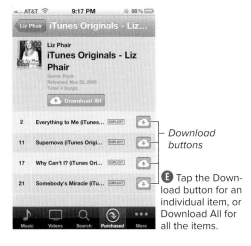

C In the iTunes app, if you choose TV Shows, you can see a list of the shows you've previously purchased.

D Since you are re-downloading, you probably want to use the Not On This iPhone category.

— Download buttons

E Tap the Download button for an individual item, or Download All for all the items.

To re-download items on iOS:

1. You re-download purchases in the iOS app that deals with the item you want to re-download. So you use the iBooks app to retrieve books from the iTunes Store; the iTunes app for Music or TV Shows; and the App Store app to re-download apps. The process is similar in all three apps. Do one or more of the following:

   In the iTunes app, tap Purchased at the bottom of the screen, then choose either Music or TV Shows **C**.

   or

   In the iBooks app, tap the Library button, tap the Store button, then tap Purchased at the bottom of the screen.

   or

   In the App Store app, tap Purchased at the bottom of the screen.

2. In the App Store and iTunes apps, tap the Not On This (*device name*) button so that you don't inadvertently re-download an item that's already on your device **D**.

3. Find the item or items that you want to re-download, then tap the download button next to the item, or the Download All button (the latter only appears in the iTunes app) **E**.

TIP It's important to note that in order to re-download items, you must be signed in to iCloud with the same Apple ID you used to purchase those items in the first place. If you want an item that was purchased under a different Apple ID (for example, my wife and I each have the other's devices authorized under our individual Apple IDs, so we can share purchases), you must sign out of iCloud on your device and sign back in using the other Apple ID.

To re-download items in iTunes:

1. In iTunes, click on the Purchased item in the sidebar.

   All the items that you purchased from the iTunes Store appear in the list .

2. Click Download Previous Purchases in the lower right corner of the window.

   iTunes connects to the iTunes Store.

3. Click the category from which you want to re-download an item (Music, TV Shows, Apps, or Books) **G**.

4. Find the item you wish to re-download, then click the Download button next to it. Alternatively, you can click the Download All button at the bottom of the window.

   iTunes downloads the selected items.

> **TIP** The Download All button is not available for TV Shows.

> **TIP** Even though you can purchase movies through the iTunes Store, you cannot re-download them.

F Choose Purchased in the iTunes sidebar to see your purchased items.

G Choose the category of the item that you wish to re-download.

ITunes Match allows you to replicate the contents of your local iTunes Library on iCloud, without the hassle of needing to upload your entire music collection.

Configuring and Using iTunes Match

iTunes in the Cloud works fine to distribute apps, books, individual music tracks, and albums you purchased from the iTunes Store to your different devices. But if, like many of us, much of your music collection comes from CDs you've ripped over the years into your iTunes Library, you probably want a way to get that music onto your devices as well. Of course, you've always been able to synchronize your music from iTunes to another device via a cable. But that requires that you know what it is that you want to synchronize before you leave on a trip, and move that music manually over to the mobile device. It would be better if you could simply download any part of your music collection to your mobile device according to your mood.

With a subscription service called iTunes Match, you can do exactly that Ⓐ. Launched initially only in the United States, iTunes Match costs $25 a year. What it does is clever: it scans all the tracks in your iTunes Library, and then matches them with the same files that are already on the iTunes Store (as of this writing, there are more than 20 million tracks in the iTunes Store). Once it matches your files with the Store's files, it shows your entire library and marks your files as downloadable on all your devices. When you want to listen to a track, iCloud uses the version from the Store, so you don't need to upload your entire music library (and saving Apple valuable server space; this way, it doesn't have to keep thousands of copies of popular songs on their servers, just the one copy from the Store). A real advantage of using iTunes Match is that matched music files that you stream or download from the

Store are in the 256 Kbps AAC format, with no DRM (Digital Rights Management). If you had previously ripped a song at a lower quality, the matched version will be sonically superior. See the "Updating Your Music with iTunes Match" section, later in this chapter.

If iTunes Match can't find a match for some of your files, it will upload the unmatched files to iCloud for use on all your devices. Neither the matched tracks nor uploaded tracks count against the 5 GB of free storage you get with iCloud.

There are some significant limitations to iTunes Match. First, as noted before, as of November 2011, the service is only available in the United States (though like most Apple services, I would expect the service to become available in other sales territories over time). Second, if you have more than 25,000 tracks in your iTunes Library, you can't use the service (there are workarounds if you split up your library). iTunes Match will only match music files that are encoded at a bit rate of 96 kbps or greater, and files that are 200 MB or smaller. Also excluded from iTunes Match: podcasts, audio books, TV shows, movies, e-books, and ringtones. However, it does work with music videos purchased from the iTunes Store.

You'll need to enable all devices you want to use with iTunes Match. First, we'll see how to enable it in iTunes on a Mac (a PC is similar), then turn the feature on using an iOS device and download music from iCloud onto the device. Finally, we'll see how you can manage your iTunes Match devices using iTunes.

iTunes Match Requirements

One interesting feature of iTunes Match is that unlike most iCloud-related services, it doesn't require Mac OS X Lion (though because it's part of iCloud, for use on iOS devices, it does need iOS 5.0.1 or later). iTunes Match works with any version of Mac OS X that supports the needed version of iTunes (10.5.1), which means that at this writing, you can use iTunes Match on Mac OS X 10.5 Leopard or later, and the hardware requirements are trivial: any Mac with an Intel or PowerPC G5 or G4 processor and 512MB of RAM.

iTunes Match

Add this computer to iCloud to share this music with your other iCloud devices.
You will also get access to your music in iCloud from this computer.

No Thanks   Add This Computer

B If you have already signed up for iTunes
Match on a different computer, click the Add This
Computer button to add it as one of your iCloud
devices.

Sign In to download from the iTunes Store
To create an Apple Account, click Create New Account

Create New Account

If you have an Apple Account (from the iTunes Store or MobileMe, for example),
enter your Apple ID and password.

Apple ID: [   ]   Example: steve@me.com

Password: [   ]   Forgot Password?

(?)   Cancel   Sign In

C Enter the Apple ID and password associated
with the iTunes Store to begin signing up for
iTunes Match.

iTunes Match

Step 1: Gathering information about your iTunes library.
Step 2: Matching your music with songs in the iTunes Store.
Step 3: Uploading artwork and remaining songs.

You can continue using iTunes while iTunes Match is in progress

Stop

D If you have a fair amount of tracks in your
iTunes Library, it could take several hours for the
scanning to complete.

To add a computer to iTunes Match:

1. In iTunes 10.5.1 or later, click iTunes
Match in the sidebar. If you haven't
yet subscribed to iTunes Match with
the Apple ID you use with the iTunes
Store, the informational screen will
have a Subscribe button **A**. Click the
Subscribe button and go through the
subscription process.

   or

   If you have already signed up for iTunes
Match, and simply want to add the
computer as one of the iTunes Match
devices, click the Add This Computer
button **B**.

2. In the resulting dialog **C**, enter your
Apple ID and password, then click the
Sign In button.

3. Once you've agreed to the iTunes
Match subscription, iTunes begins scanning your iTunes Library and uploading
information about the tracks within it to
iCloud **D**.

   This process can take quite a while (up
to several hours), depending on how
many tracks you have in your iTunes
Library. However, you can still continue
using iTunes during the process.

continues on next page

4. Once iTunes has finished scanning your tracks, it begins matching your music with music on the iTunes Store **E**.

Again, this is usually a lengthy process, but you don't have to stop using iTunes. If you are using iTunes for something else, you can tell that the matching process is still going on because an activity icon will appear next to iTunes Match in the sidebar **F**.

5. When iTunes finishes the matching, it automatically uploads unmatched songs and their artwork to iCloud. When the whole process is complete, iTunes lets you know in the iTunes Match screen **G**. In the sidebar, a cloud icon will also appear next to the Music entry **H**.

iCloud Icons

The other icons that can appear in the iCloud Download column besides the Download icon are:

- **Ineligible** ⬡ For songs that are too large, podcasts, audio books, and songs recorded at too low a bit rate.

- **Removed** ⊗ Shown when a song has been removed from iCloud from a different computer. Songs deleted from iCloud are immediately deleted from iOS devices, but remain on other computers until they are manually deleted.

- **Error** ① Displayed when there was a problem matching the file.

- **Duplicate** ⬡ You'll see this icon when a duplicate version of the song exists in your iTunes library. The icon will appear next to duplicates that weren't uploaded to iCloud.

- **Waiting** ☁ iTunes shows this icon when a song is in the process of being matched.

E Similarly, once the scan is complete, it could take quite a while to match your local files with files in the iTunes Store.

F While the matching process is going on, you can continue using iTunes; the working icon next to iTunes Match lets you know things are still working.

G When the process is complete, iTunes tells you how many songs are now available in iCloud.

H Once your songs are available in iCloud, an iCloud icon appears next to the Music entry in the iTunes sidebar.

I To see what's going on with individual tracks, turn on iCloud Download and iCloud Status in iTunes' View Options.

J In the iTunes list, you can see which songs need to be downloaded to your local computer, as well as each track's iCloud status.

K Select all the files that need to be downloaded, then right-click and choose Download from the shortcut menu to download them to your computer.

TIP If you want to see the iTunes Match status of the items within your music library, in iTunes, choose View > View Options, then select the iCloud Download and iCloud Status checkboxes **I**, then click OK. In the Library list, iTunes will show you which items have been matched, which have been purchased, and which items are not on your current computer but are able to be downloaded from iCloud **J**. If there is no icon in the iCloud Download column, that means a copy of the track is already stored locally.

TIP To download items from iCloud, select the items in the iCloud Download column of the iTunes list with the download icon, then right-click and choose Download **K**.

TIP On a computer, if you play music that is on iCloud, iCloud will stream the music to you. On an iOS device, playing music stored on iCloud also downloads that track to your device.

To add an iOS device to iTunes Match:

1. On your iOS device, tap Settings > Music .

2. Turn on iTunes Match.

3. Your device will ask for your Apple ID Password. Enter it, then tap OK.

   The Music app warns you that iTunes Match will replace the music library on the device **M**. However, any tracks already on the device that were previously synced from iTunes will still remain on the device.

4. Tap Enable.

5. Back in the Music screen, a new option, Show All Music, will appear. Turn this on to get access to your entire iCloud music library.

TIP When you know you won't have access to your online iCloud library (say, while you are on a plane flight), switching the **Show All Music** option to **Off** tells your iOS device to only show locally stored music.

L Begin enabling iTunes Match in the Music section of the Settings app.

M When you turn on iTunes Match, iOS 5 warns you that it will replace the music library on the device.

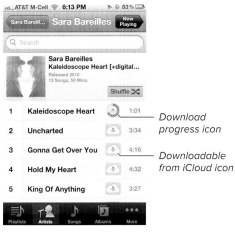

When you download a track from iCloud, it begins playing before it has completed downloading.

Begin managing your iTunes Match devices in the iTunes Manage Accounts screen.

On the Manage Devices screen, you can see which computers and iOS devices are associated with iTunes Match, and you can remove them if needed.

To download music from iCloud to your iOS device:

1. In the Music app, the Playlists, Artists, Songs, and Albums tabs will now show everything in your iTunes Library. Navigate to music that you would like to download from iCloud to your device. You can tell that a track is not stored locally because it will have the iCloud Download icon next to it.

2. Tap the iCloud Download icon to begin downloading the track. After a moment, the track will begin downloading and playing, and a progress icon appears next to the track name .

   or

   Scroll down to the end of the album tracks and tap the Download All icon.

To manage iTunes Match devices:

1. In iTunes, click iTunes Store in the sidebar.

2. In the upper right corner of the iTunes window, click your Apple ID to access your account information.

3. Enter your Apple ID and password when prompted, then click View Account.

4. In the Account Information screen, there will be a section called iTunes in the Cloud .

5. Click Manage Devices.

6. The resulting screen will show you the devices associated with iTunes in the Cloud. If you want to remove one of these devices, click the Remove button next to it, then click Done.

TIP Apple allows you to associate a particular device or computer with a different Apple ID only once every 90 days.

Updating Your Music with iTunes Match

As mentioned earlier, once iTunes Match scans your music library, it matches the songs that it finds with versions of the same track in the iTunes Store. You can then replace the versions on your computer (which may have been ripped from CD with old programs at lower-quality bit rates; I found a bunch of my music was originally ripped at 128 Kbps with Sound-Jam, the program Apple purchased and turned into iTunes back in 2000!) with new, higher-quality 256 Kbps AAC formatted files. If you previously purchased copy-protected music from the iTunes Store, the replacement tracks will not only be higher quality, but will no longer have copy protection. If you don't want to invest in iTunes Match, Apple provides a service that allows you to update older-quality files you purchased from the Store to iTunes Plus (that 256 Kbps AAC format) for $.30 per track. Of course, if you want to upgrade more than 83 songs, it makes better financial sense to subscribe to iTunes Match.

To replace the older files with newer versions from the iTunes Store, you need to first find lower-quality versions of music in your library. A great tool to do that in iTunes is a Smart Playlist. Then you need to delete the old files from your library, and finally redownload the improved-quality versions from iCloud to your local library. I'd like to acknowledge Jason Snell, editorial director of *Macworld* magazine, for his excellent article detailing this process, which you can find at `http://www.macworld.com/article/163620/2011/11/how_to_upgrade_tracks_to_itunes_match_fast.html`. I've built on his work here.

TIP In the *Macworld* article referenced above, the author suggests you just replace all of your lesser-quality files in one massive operation. I don't recommend that, because in my experience, iTunes Match's matching, while quite good, isn't yet perfect. See the "It's Good, But It Ain't Gospel" sidebar.

Add criterion

Q Begin creating your Smart Playlist to root out your files that are good candidates for upgrading to higher quality.

R These criteria look for lower-bit rate music.

To find matched songs that need upgrading:

1. Open iTunes.

2. Choose File > New Smart Playlist.

   The Smart Playlist window appears **Q**.

3. Change the first criterion. From the first pop-up menu, choose "Media Kind."

   The other two pop-up menus on that line will change to "is" and "Music." That's what we want.

4. Click the plus button at the right edge of the first criterion to add another criterion.

5. In the new criterion, change the first pop-up menu to "Bit Rate," the middle pop-up menu to "is less than," and enter "256" in the Kbps field **R**.

6. Now we want to create a criterion group, where multiple criteria are treated as though they were one. To do that, hold down the Option key and click the Add criterion button for the criterion you created in Step 5.

   The new criterion group appears, with the pop-up menu set to "All" of the following are true, and one sub-criterion ready to be set.

7. In that pop-up menu, change "All" to "Any."

8. In the first pop-up menu of the sub-criterion, choose " iCloud Status."

   The other two pop-up menus of the sub-criterion will change to "is" and "Matched," which is what we want.

   continues on next page

9. In the first sub-criterion, click its Add criterion button to add a new line to the group.

10. In the first pop-up menu of the new sub-criterion, choose " iCloud Status" again, leave the second pop-up menu set to "is," and change the third pop-up menu to "Purchased."

11. (Optional) Select the Match only checked items checkbox.

12. Select the Live updating checkbox.

The settings for your Smart Playlist should now look like ⑤.

13. Click OK.

The new Smart Playlist appears in the iTunes sidebar with the name "untitled playlist."

14. Click the words "untitled playlist," and change the name of the playlist to "Better Quality on iCloud."

⑤ The final Smart Playlist settings.

T iTunes always asks if you're sure you want to get rid of items.

U Here, you want to delete the local, lower-quality copies of your songs, so click Delete Files.

✓	Baba O'Riley	⊙ ☁ Matched	5:00	The Who	Who's Next
✓	Bargain	⊙ ☁ Matched	5:34	The Who	Who's Next
✓	Love Ain't for Keepin'	⊙ ☁ Matched	2:11	The Who	Who's Next
✓	My Wife	⊙ ☁ Matched	3:36	The Who	Who's Next
✓	The Song is Over	⊙ ☁ Matched	6:18	The Who	Who's Next
✓	Gettin' In Tune	⊙ ☁ Matched	4:49	The Who	Who's Next
✓	Goin' Mobile	⊙ ☁ Matched	3:43	The Who	Who's Next
✓	Behind Blue Eyes	⊙ ☁ Matched	3:41	The Who	Who's Next
✓	Won't Get Fooled Again	⊙ ☁ Matched	8:32	The Who	Who's Next

V Once you delete local files, the iCloud download icon appears next to them, indicating that the songs are waiting for you in the cloud.

To replace your lower-bit rate music with higher-quality versions from iCloud:

1. In the iTunes sidebar, click the "Better Quality on iCloud" Smart Playlist you just created.

   The playlist shows a list of lower-quality tracks that iTunes Match has matched and thinks are upgradable to better quality.

2. In the list, select one or more songs that you want to replace.

3. Press Option-Delete.

   iTunes will ask if you're sure if you want to delete the songs from your library **T**. Make sure that you *do not check* "Also delete these items from iCloud."

4. Click Delete Items.

   iTunes will ask if you want to keep the local files in the iTunes Media folder **U**. Scary as it may feel, yes, you do. The tracks are still available for you to redownload from iCloud, which you'll be doing soon.

5. Click Delete Files.

   iTunes deletes the local files, and marks the items with the iCloud download icon, showing that the files are now available on iCloud, rather than in your local library **V**.

6. Select the files you just deleted, then right-click and choose Download from the shortcut menu.

   iTunes downloads the higher-quality files from the iTunes Store.

It's Good, But It Ain't Gospel

iTunes Match is a surprisingly good service, but its matching (at this writing, at least) is far from perfect. It seems to often fall down on older and obscure albums, especially if they aren't in the iTunes Store.

Here are some examples from my own experience. In my iTunes Library, I have three CDs from a folk duo called The Williams Brothers that were made between 1987 through 1993. Only one of these three CDs is in the iTunes Store. Once you do a match, you can ask iTunes to show you the matched track on the Store. For one of these albums, it shows a match to a completely unrelated group called The Glass Brothers **W**. For another CD (the one that happens to be in the Store), it shows a match to The Williams Brothers, a famous vocal group of three black gospel singers **X**.

Online reports (corroborated by my own experience) suggest some other problems:

- Sometimes, songs within the same CD don't always match. This is puzzling, to say the least. iTunes will upload the tracks that don't match from your local copies, but it's still weird behavior.

- It's unclear what version of a track you may get if there are multiple versions of the track available on the Store (for example, original and remastered).

- Sometimes artwork isn't transferred to tracks that are downloaded.

These issues may be teething pains in the early days of iTunes Match. After all, as I write this, the feature has only been publicly available for less than a week (those pesky deadlines!). But I still recommend caution before trying a wholesale conversion of older files to your library to new versions. It's not a bad idea to spot-check that matched tracks are correct before upgrading them.

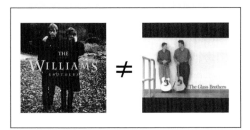

W These aren't the droids we're looking for.

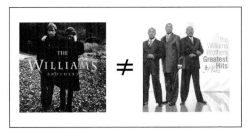

X This was another incorrect iTunes Match. The folk singers on the left just don't have the gospel spirit of the group on the right.

Backing up to iCloud

Before the advent of iCloud, backing up an iOS device meant physically connecting it to a computer running iTunes via a USB cable, then letting that connection make a copy of the contents of the device onto your computer. iCloud eliminates the need for that cable, because it allows you to backup the data on your iOS device over a Wi-Fi connection to the iCloud servers. It's your choice: you can back up over Wi-Fi, or continue your backups via a direct connection to your computer. Naturally, if disaster strikes, you can also restore your data to an iOS device from a previous iCloud backup.

If iCloud's free 5 GB of storage aren't enough for you, you can manage the amount of data stored in the cloud, and even purchase more storage if needed.

In This Chapter

Understanding and Configuring iCloud Backup

Everyone knows you should back up the data on your computers and mobile devices in case of hardware failure or theft. The problem is that unless the process is made incredibly easy (as in set it and forget it) most people simply don't back up their stuff. Apple has tried to solve the backup problem with the Mac with Time Machine, and with the introduction of iCloud, backing up your iOS device can now be done wirelessly and automatically, as long as you set it up once.

As part of its synchronization process, iTunes has always backed up your data when you connect your iOS device with a USB cable. Now, Apple uses iCloud to backup your data over Wi-Fi, and all you have to do to make the backup happen is turn it on once, either in iTunes or on your iOS device, be on a Wi-Fi network, connect the device to a power source (which you have to do to recharge the battery anyway), and not be using the device for a while.

Before we jump into setting it up, let's talk for a moment about what gets backed up. Some of the items that are backed up count against the free 5 GB of storage you get with an iCloud account, and some items do not.

Items that count against the 5 GB of free iCloud storage:

- Data kept inside apps. For example, I have the Amazon Kindle app on my iPad. I have about 60 MB worth of books loaded in the app. That counts against part of my 5 GB storage quota.

- Photos and videos in the Camera Roll.
- Messages, such as SMS, MMS, and iMessages.
- Device settings, such as Mail, Contacts, and Calendar accounts.
- Home screen and app organization information.
- Ringtones.

You get unlimited free storage for:

- Music, apps, books, and TV shows that you purchased from the iTunes Store.
- Items that are in your Photo Stream.

Things that *don't* get backed up to iCloud include:

- Music and TV shows you didn't buy from the iTunes Store (though if you subscribe to iTunes Match, music you didn't buy from the iTunes Store may still be available on iCloud, but it won't get backed up, and won't count against your storage quota).
- Movies.
- Podcasts and audio books.
- Photos that were originally synced from your computer (instead of using Photo Stream).

Your first backup could take a while, depending on how much data is on your mobile device that needs backing up. Because iCloud Backup is smart, subsequent backups only copy items that have been added or changed, so those subsequent backups go much quicker.

After the first backup, the backup happens automatically once a day, when the device is connected to the Internet over Wi-Fi, is connected to a power source, and the screen is locked.

So now we know what does and doesn't get backed up, and when the backups happen, let's set up your device for automatic backup, so you need never worry about it again.

To turn on iCloud Backup on an iOS device:

1. Choose Settings > iCloud > Storage & Backup.

2. In the Backup section, turn on iCloud Backup **A**.

3. In the resulting dialog, tap OK to confirm you want to use iCloud Backup.

4. (Optional) Scroll down on the Storage & Backup screen and tap the Back Up Now button to begin your first backup. Make sure you're connected to a power source and to Wi-Fi.

To turn on iCloud Backup in iTunes:

1. Connect the iOS device to iTunes, then select the device in the sidebar.

2. In the Backup section of the Summary screen, select the Back up to iCloud button **B**.

TIP Once you turn on iCloud Backup, iTunes no longer backs up your iOS device when you sync; it all happens in the cloud.

A Turn on iCloud Backup to begin backing up your iOS device via Wi-Fi to Apple's servers.

B In iTunes, you can choose to either backup to iCloud or to the local computer.

Set Up iPhone

Choose to set up as a new iPhone or restore from a backup.

Set Up as New iPhone

Restore from iCloud Backup ✓

Restore from iTunes Backup

Ⓐ The Setup Assistant gives you the opportunity to restore from an iCloud Backup.

Restoring an iOS Device from Backup

Restoring an iOS device from a backup is a bit weird. You have very little control over the process. You can only restore to an iOS device that has been wiped clean or is brand-new. The restoration happens as part of the Setup Assistant on a new iOS 5 device.

To restore from an iCloud Backup:

1. On an erased or new iOS device, turn it on. The Setup Assistant will automatically run.

2. When you get to the Set Up (*device name*) screen, you'll have the option to Restore from iCloud Backup. Tap that choice Ⓐ, then enter your Apple ID and password.

3. From the next screen, which shows the three most recent backups for each of your backup devices, choose the backup you wish to use for the restore, then tap Restore.

   The backup will be downloaded, after which your device will restart and restore your settings and data.

Managing Your iCloud Storage

You have some control over the amount of storage that you're using iCloud. From the iCloud preference pane on Mac or the iCloud control panel on Windows, you can view how much storage you're using from your free 5 GB allocation, choose to remove some data to free up space, and purchase more iCloud storage space.

Remember, music, apps, books, and TV shows that you purchased from the iTunes Store, and photos in your Photo Stream, don't count against your 5 GB of free storage.

To manage your iCloud storage on a computer:

1. Choose System Preferences > iCloud on the Mac.

   or

   Choose Start Menu > Control Panel > iCloud on Windows.

   The iCloud settings window appears **A**. At the bottom of the settings window, there is a bar graph showing you how much iCloud storage you have available.

2. Click Manage.

   The Manage Storage pane appears **B**. On the left, it lists the different categories of storage you are using in iCloud, and how much space each category is using.

3. Click a category to see the documents within it **C**.

Available storage

A Begin managing your iCloud storage on the Mac in the iCloud pane of System Preferences.

B You can see what is taking up room in your iCloud storage in the Manage Storage pane.

C Clicking one of the categories shows you its details.

Keynote for iPad Project File.key–tef	7.1 MB
NZ Trip Presentation.key–tef	6.3 MB
Partner Presentation.key–tef	4 MB
College Presentation.key–tef	3 MB
Healdsburg Tourism.key–tef	11.7 MB
JS Video Presentation	1.6 MB
Pages Session.key–tef	1.6 MB
Motion Paths X.key–tef	779.2 KB
Bullets.key–tef	630.3 KB
Dreamweaver CS5 Preso.key–tef	513.8 KB

Delete   Additional data: 504.2 KB   Delete All

Done

D Select an item and click Delete to remove it from iCloud.

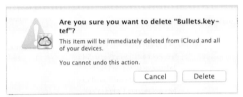

Are you sure you want to delete "Bullets.key–tef"?

This item will be immediately deleted from iCloud and all of your devices.

You cannot undo this action.

Cancel   Delete

E If you're not sure you want to get rid of that item, this is the time to click the Cancel button.

4. If you want to delete one of the items within the category, click to select it, then click Delete **D**.

or

If you want to delete all of the items within the category, click Delete All.

iCloud asks if you are certain you wish to delete, and warns you that the item will be immediately deleted from iCloud and your devices **E**.

5. Click Delete.

The item is deleted and you'll return to the Manage Storage pane.

6. Click Done.

To manage your iCloud storage on an iOS device:

1. Tap Settings > iCloud.

2. At the bottom of the list, tap Storage & Backup .

3. On the Storage & Backup screen , tap Manage Storage.

   On the Manage Storage screen, the categories of storage you're using appears .

F On an iOS device, begin managing your storage in the iCloud portion of Settings.

G Next, in the Storage & Backup screen, tap Manage Storage.

H The Manage Storage screen shows you how your iCloud storage is distributed.

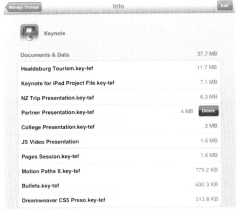

I You can turn back up on or off for individual apps on your device.

J If you like, you can delete individual files from iCloud.

4. (Optional) On an iOS device, you have a bit more granular control over the storage used for backups on that particular device. In the Backups section of the Manage Storage screen, tap the backup for the iOS device you are working with to choose backup options for the apps you are backing up **I**. If you want to stop backing up data for a particular app, simply turn it off under the Backup Options section.

5. Tap a category to see the documents within it.

6. To delete a particular item, swipe a finger to the right on the item to make the Delete button appear **J**, then tap Delete.

To purchase more iCloud storage:

1. Choose System Preferences > iCloud on the Mac.

   or

   Choose Start Menu > Control Panel > iCloud on Windows.

   The iCloud settings window appears.

2. Click Manage.

   The Manage Storage pane appears.

3. Click Buy More Storage.

   In the resulting dialog **K**, choose the amount of storage upgrade you wish, then click Next.

   Your storage upgrade will be charged to your iTunes account and go into effect immediately, and will automatically renew each year unless you downgrade to the free storage plan before your renewal date. Once you upgrade your plan, if you decide you made a mistake, you can get a full refund within 15 days of an upgrade, or within 45 days after a yearly payment.

TIP To purchase more iCloud storage on an iOS device, tap Settings > iCloud, then tap the Buy More Storage button. In the resulting dialog **L**, you'll get the same storage upgrade options. Choose the option you want, then tap the Buy button.

K You can use the iCloud preference pane on Mac or the iCloud control panel on Windows to purchase more storage.

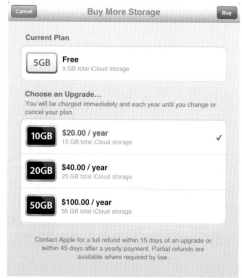

L You can also purchase more iCloud storage on an iOS device.

Synchronizing Browser Bookmarks

We all use bookmarks to make our web browsing experience easier, but it can be kind of a pain to be working on one device, and realize that you bookmarked a particular site on another device. Relax; iCloud has you covered. It can synchronize browser bookmarks across four different browsers: Safari for Mac and Windows, Safari for iOS, and Microsoft's Internet Explorer for Windows.

With bookmark synchronization, any changes you make to your bookmarks on one device are pushed to your other devices, and the bookmark set up on each device is merged. You can choose to turn on bookmark synchronization between a subset of your devices, or all of them.

In this chapter, you'll see how to turn on bookmark synchronization and learn a little about the best ways to manage bookmarks. As a bonus, I'll point you to some useful bookmarklets, which are little, handy JavaScript programs masquerading as everyday bookmarks.

About Bookmark Management

If you're anything like me, you have a huge selection of bookmarks that you've created over the years, on different computers and different devices, and the thought of having iCloud merge them all together onto all of your devices is a bit daunting. That's why I think it's a good idea to do a little preparation before you turn on browser synchronization.

- **Do some spring cleaning.** If possible, get all your devices in one place. This is a good time to compare and review bookmarks on your devices and get rid of duplicates and outdated bookmarks. Your goal is to keep only the bookmarks that are still useful. If you bookmarked a particular page that has an article on it that you want to read, go ahead and read it, or save it to one of the read-later services, such as Instapaper (**www.instapaper.com**) or Readability (**www.readability.com**). After you've dealt with the article, delete the bookmark.

- **Decide which devices you want to synchronize.** After thinking about it a little, I realized that I had no real interest in synchronizing all of the bookmarks on my desktop and laptop computers with each other, much less with my mobile devices. I tend to use the desktop in my office for different purposes than the laptop, and I use Safari on my iOS devices (my iPad and my iPhone) in similar ways, but differently than how I use bookmarks with my Macs. So I decided to merge and synchronize my bookmarks only between my mobile devices, leaving the feature turned off on my Macs and on my Windows machine.

A On a Mac, you turn on Bookmarks synchronization from the iCloud preference pane.

B On Windows, you use the iCloud control panel.

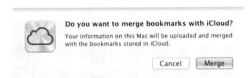

Do you want to merge bookmarks with iCloud?

Your information on this Mac will be uploaded and merged with the bookmarks stored in iCloud.

Cancel   Merge

C As usual, iCloud warns you before you do something that might change data across many devices.

D On Windows, you can choose whether you want to use iCloud bookmarks with Internet Explorer or Safari for Windows.

Configuring Bookmark Syncing with iCloud

Once you've cleaned up your bookmarks and decided which devices you want to synchronize, turning bookmark synchronization on is easy. Just follow these steps:

To enable bookmark synchronization on a Mac or Windows machine:

1. (Mac) Choose System Preferences, then click the iCloud icon.

    The iCloud preferences appear **A**.

    or

    (Windows) Choose Start Menu > Control Panel, click the Network and Internet section, then click iCloud.

    The iCloud control panel appears **B**.

2. Click the checkbox next to Bookmarks.

    iCloud asks if you're sure you want to merge bookmarks **C**.

3. Click Merge.

TIP On Windows, there is an Options button in the control panel; clicking this allows you to choose if you want to merge your bookmarks from Internet Explorer, or Safari for Windows **D**.

To enable bookmark synchronization on an iOS device:

1. Tap Settings, then iCloud.

   The iCloud settings appear 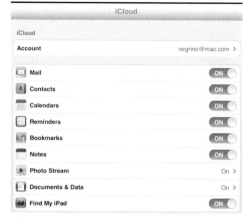.

2. Slide the Bookmarks switch to On.

   Your device warns you that you're about to merge your bookmarks with iCloud **F**.

3. Click Merge.

   After the merge is complete, the same bookmarks will appear on all enabled devices. Changes made on one device will be replicated on the other devices on your iCloud account.

> **TIP** Some folders' contents are synchronized, but the folders can't be deleted, notably the History, Bookmarks Bar, and Bookmarks Menu folders. That's true even on the iPhone and iPhone touch, which don't have a Bookmarks Bar.

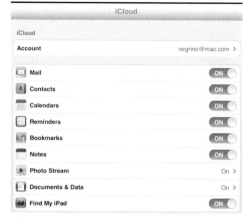

E You turn Bookmarks synchronization on in the iCloud settings on iOS.

F On a mobile device, you get the same warning that your data will be merged.

Useful Bookmarklets for iOS

Bookmarklets are bookmarks (or favorites, if you prefer Internet Explorer's terminology) that contain a small JavaScript program, rather than a URL. When you tap the bookmarklet, it executes the JavaScript program.

I like to use bookmarklets on my iOS devices because they can often substitute for a feature that most desktop browsers (including Safari for the Mac) have and mobile Safari does not: browser extensions. For example, on the desktop I have browser extensions installed that clip web content to my snippet manager of choice, Evernote (from the company of the same name; **www.evernote.com**), and re-style pages that are designed in such a way that I find them difficult to read (what is it with designers who like little white type on dark backgrounds?).

In this section, I'm going to point you to three bookmarklets that you'll be able to download from the book's website at www.peachpit.com/icloudvqs, and show you how to install them into your iCloud-enabled browsers. There are, of course, many more bookmarklets available.

- **Unicode Symbols** gives you a new browser window or tab that allows you to copy and paste useful symbols that are not possible to type from the iOS keyboard.

- **Black Text** makes the background of a web page white and the text on the page black. I use it to make overly designed pages more legible.

- **Clip to Evernote** brings up a window that allows you to send the current selection to the free Evernote clipping service.

Safari for Mac and iPad have a Bookmarks Bar that allow easy access to frequently used bookmarks. With their smaller screen real estate, the iPhone and iPod touch lack the Bookmarks Bar.

Something you should know about installing bookmarklets: it's *way* easier to do it on the Mac or PC, then synchronize it with your mobile device via iCloud. On a computer, all you need to do is drag a link containing the bookmarklet to the Bookmarks Bar, then name the bookmarklet. On an iOS device, it's a complicated procedure, which I've detailed below on an iPad. Follow it carefully, and here's hoping that Apple makes it easier to add bookmarklets in the future.

In Safari on iOS, copy and paste the contents of the boxes below, according to the detailed instructions in the book:

Unicode symbols:

A In order to use a Bookmarklet on iOS, you'll need to copy the code in this text box.

B Tapping twice brings up the Edit popover so you can tap Select All.

Unicode symbols:

C After the selection, the Edit popover changes to show you the Copy option.

D You need to add a bookmark from the Actions button.

To add a bookmarklet on an iOS device:

1. In Safari on your mobile device, go to the book's web page at **www.peachpit.com/icloudvqs**.

2. On the page, the JavaScript code for each bookmarklet is in a text box **A**. Tap inside a text box, pause for a second, then tap again. In the Edit popover, tap Select All **B**, then tap Copy **C**.

3. In the toolbar, tap the Actions button 🖪, then tap Add Bookmark from the resulting popover **D**.

4. In the Add Bookmark popover **E**, change *Untitled* to the name of the bookmarklet you are creating.

   The address for the bookmark below the name shows the URL of the Peachpit page. We'll change that in a moment; it can't be changed yet.

5. Below the URL, choose the location where you want the bookmarklet (I usually use the Bookmarks Bar), then tap Save.

continues on next page

E Change the default Untitled name to the name of the bookmarklet you are creating.

6. Tap the Bookmarks button in the toolbar, and locate the newly created bookmark. Tap Edit ❶.

The screen changes to the edit mode ❷.

7. Tap the bookmark name (make sure not to tap the "Delete" or "Move" controls) to select it for editing.

The popover changes to Edit Bookmark, with the Peachpit URL.

8. Tap the URL, then tap the X "Clearcontents" control, tap again in the Address line to invoke the Edit popover, then tap Paste ❸.

The JavaScript code you copied in Step 2 is pasted in the Address line.

9. Tap outside the Edit Bookmark popover to save your changes. The new bookmarklet appears in the Bookmarks Bar ❹ on the iPad, or wherever else you put it in your Bookmarks.

10. To run the bookmarklet, tap it in the Bookmarks Bar, or choose it from your Bookmarks.

For the Unicode Symbols bookmarklet, the symbols appear in a new tab ❺; you can copy a symbol from the window and paste it wherever you need it.

❶ After finding the bookmark you just created, tap Edit.

Move
Delete

❷ Tap the name of the bookmark to edit it.

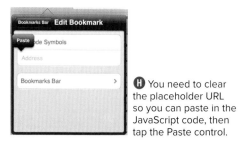

❸ You need to clear the placeholder URL so you can paste in the JavaScript code, then tap the Paste control.

❹ The new bookmarklet appears in the Bookmarks Bar on the iPad.

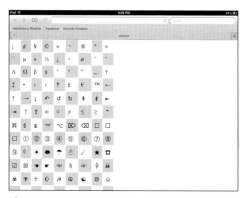

❺ For the Unicode Symbols example, copy the symbol you want from the page, then paste it into any other application.

9

Working with Documents in the Cloud

A real problem with using many devices is that it's surprisingly easy to work on a project and lose track of a document, or worse, its latest version. For example, I'm writing this chapter in Microsoft Word 2011 on the MacBook on my kitchen table. Later, I'll save and close the chapter, go up to my office, and continue working on the Mac Pro. If I wanted to, I could even be a huge cliché, head over to Starbucks, and write on my iPad, using a Word-compatible app.

I can work on one document across all devices because my Word file is in a folder using the free Dropbox service, which automatically keeps it synchronized and available everywhere. But I still have to worry about where the document is (it has to be in Dropbox), and saving it. It would be even better if the document would auto-save and push its latest version to my devices. That's the aim of iCloud's Documents in the Cloud feature.

In This Chapter

Configuring Documents in the Cloud

Before we get into the details of Documents in the Cloud, let's define what it is (and what it isn't), at least as of the Fall of 2011, when I'm writing this.

- **What it is:** A good way to work on iWork documents between iOS devices and (to a lesser extent) your Macs. As you work on an iWork document on iOS, it is, like all iOS documents, automatically saved in a mysterious location that you don't have explicit access to (because iOS hides the file system from the user). When Documents in the Cloud is enabled, iCloud automatically pushes the latest version to your other iOS devices, though you must manually download the changed version to your Macs from iCloud.com. Since the concept of a file system is foreign to iOS (each program has its private "bucket" of documents), we'll eventually have to see some standardized way that programs with both Mac and iOS versions can access the same files, but that doesn't exist yet.

  You can also think of Documents in the Cloud as an invisible and seamless way of backing up your iWork documents, since they are sent to iCloud as soon as you change them. As a facilitator of your work between iOS devices, Documents in the Cloud works quite well. You can start a document on your iPhone as inspiration strikes, then continue working on it on your iPad, and you'll pick up right where you left off.

  As more developers build Documents in the Cloud into their apps (as I write this, there are very few), it will become increasingly more useful beyond the iWork realm.

- **What it isn't:** A general automatic file synchronization service. For Documents in the Cloud to work, the developer needs to enable it in their app, and it is really intended to support iOS, more than Mac OS X or Windows. If you're more interested in a general sync service that works across many platforms, including Mac OS X, iOS, and Windows, there are many, including Dropbox (**www.dropbox.com**), Sugar-Sync (**www.sugarsync.com**), and Box. net (**www.box.net**). These services also allow you to set one or more individual folders for synchronization between devices, using the familiar file system metaphor of files and folders. What you don't get with a general service that you do get with iCloud is the automatic updating of documents (iWork or otherwise) across mobile devices (though some of these services offer automatic synchronization on desktop operating systems). That's a manual process if you use one of these services. Documents in the Cloud is also emphatically not a competitor to online document creation services like Google Docs. There's no website where you can create documents that then are synchronized via Documents in the Cloud.

Any documents that you synchronize using Documents in the Cloud count against your free 5 GB iCloud storage quota.

Documents in the Cloud also includes and synchronizes app data between your mobile devices. For example, a game that's been written to be universal (meaning it plays on both the iPad and smaller-screened iOS devices) and has been updated to take advantage of Documents in the Cloud can automatically synchronize its game data using iCloud, so you could play a few levels of the game on one device, and continue playing the game at the same point you left off on another device (many games use Apple's Game Center, which is part of iOS, to achieve the same goals).

TIP Because Keynote documents can contain large files, especially graphics, it's a good idea to make them as small as possible before you move them to iOS devices, in order to save both space on your devices and to minimize the impact on your iCloud storage quota. Before you upload a Keynote presentation from your Mac to iCloud.com (where it will be pushed automatically to your iOS devices), in Keynote for Mac, choose File > Reduce File Size. This command resamples the graphics in your presentation to screen resolution, greatly reducing their size.

TIP Don't forget that the versions of the iWork programs for iOS still have a subset of the features of iWork for Mac. So there could be some aspects of your documents (for example, certain slide builds or transition effects in Keynote) that don't survive a round trip journey from your Mac through iCloud to Keynote for iOS and back.

Deathmatch: iCloud versus Dropbox

The Dropbox service gives you 2 GB of free storage (you can purchase more storage for a fee) that you can access from all your devices, be they desktop, laptop, or mobile. The idea behind Dropbox is simple: when you install the program, it creates a Dropbox folder (typically on your desktop). Then, any file that you save to your is Dropbox automatically copied to all your computers, phones and iPads (items are copied to mobile devices on demand to save bandwidth), and the Dropbox website. You can have any mix of files and folders inside your Dropbox folder, and you can choose to share any of those with anyone else, without them sharing all of your other stuff.

For me, Dropbox has become an integral part of my workflow. I keep all of my current project files in folders inside my Dropbox folder, and I know then that I'm always working with the latest version of my files. I even use Dropbox to transfer files between two machines that are physically right next to each other, because I don't need to worry about doing the transfer; it just happens by itself. Throughout this book, you've seen the results of this process; when I grab a screenshot of the iCloud control panel on Windows, my screenshot program is set to save the image to my Dropbox folder, and a couple of seconds after I snap the image, it automatically appears on my Mac a foot away, which is where I do cropping, add callouts, and the like. The Dropbox website also remembers past versions of documents, and I can revert to an older version, or restore a document that I inadvertantly deleted.

Compared to the flexibility I get from Dropbox, iCloud's Documents in the Cloud isn't yet a serious competitor. It's nice that I can start working on a Pages document or Keynote presentation on my iPhone and have it automatically pushed to my iPad, but that's just not the same as being able to open a document on *any* computer or mobile device and know that I'm working with the latest version and that I don't have to worry about file management. Until Documents in the Cloud becomes more ubiquitous and flexible, I don't think that any of the general file synchronization services have that much to worry about.

To enable Documents in the Cloud on Mac:

1. Choose System Preferences, then click the iCloud icon.

   The iCloud preferences appear Ⓐ.

2. Click the checkbox next to Documents & Data.

To enable Documents in the Cloud on iOS:

1. Tap Settings, then iCloud.

   The iCloud settings appear Ⓑ.

2. Tap Documents & Data Ⓒ.

3. On the resulting screen Ⓓ, slide the Documents & Data switch to On.

4. (Optional) If you want to allow your documents and data to synchronize over the cellular data network, slide the Use Cellular switch to On.

   If you have bandwidth caps and you regularly transfer a lot of cellular data, you might want to leave this option turned Off.

Ⓐ On the Mac, you'll turn on Documents in the Cloud in the iCloud preference pane.

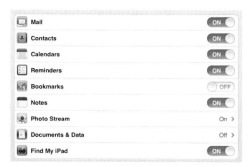

Ⓑ On iOS, you'll use the Documents & Data section of the iCloud Settings.

Ⓒ When you switch Documents & Data on, iCloud will begin synchronizing your iWork documents to the iCloud servers.

Ⓓ You can choose whether or not you want to use cellular data networks to synchronize your document and other data.

E The iCloud settings for the iWork applications are in the system Settings app (this one is for Pages).

F Some App makers prefer to keep their settings inside their apps, as with the iCloud settings shown here for GoodReader, an excellent app that lets you read, annotate, and manage PDF, office, iWork, and even image and video files.

G Here are Keynote presentation files that were on my iPad in the process of being updated on my iPhone via iCloud.

5. (Optional) Some of your apps (for example, the iWork apps for iOS) may have Use iCloud switches in their sections in the Settings app **E**. You may need to turn these on. Other apps won't use the Settings app for their settings, but will contain their settings within the app itself **F**.

TIP After you turn on Documents in the Cloud, if you take a look at the Document Managers in the iWork programs, you can see the files being updated **G**. After updating, you can work with them as usual **H**.

H This Keynote file started life on my Mac, then was transferred to the iPad, where it got a few touch-ups before the presentation.

Working with iWork Documents on the iCloud Website

In order to get iWork files from your Mac into iCloud, where they will then be automatically distributed to your iOS devices, you need to use the iCloud website. Conversely, you can access files that are already in iCloud on a computer through the web interface, and download them to your computer. The iCloud website allows you to download or upload the files onto your computers in one of the iWork formats (Keynote, Pages, or Numbers); Microsoft Office formats (PowerPoint, Word, or Excel); or as a PDF.

It's important to remember that files that you get from iCloud and then update on your computer are not automatically updated on iCloud and your mobile devices. To deal with your files on a computer, it's a manual process of uploading and downloading using the website.

To manage iWork files on the iCloud website:

1. Go to the iCloud website, and login using your iCloud Apple ID and password.

2. On the iCloud Home screen **A**, click iWork.

   The iWork screen appears **B**.

A Begin managing your files on your computer on the iCloud website.

Keynote presentation file | iWork program tabs

Actions

Folder

B The iWork screen shows you all of your iWork documents that have been uploaded to iCloud.

C Choose the download format you want.

D You can also manage your iWork files with the pop-up menu from the Actions button.

E This dialog also allows you to choose your preferred download format.

F Drag the iWork file you want to upload from your desktop into the iWork browser window.

3. At the top of the window, click the tab for the iWork program you wish to work with.

4. Do one of the following:

▸ To download a file to your computer, click on the file, and a Download button appears. Click the Download button, and choose the format you want the download to be in from the pop-up menu **C**. You can also download a file by selecting the file, clicking the Actions button, and choosing Download *filetype* from the pop-up menu **D**. You'll get a dialog that allows you to choose the download format **E**.

▸ To upload a file from your computer to iCloud, drag the file from your desktop into the iWork website window **F**, or click the Actions button, and choose Upload *filetype* from the pop-up menu.

▸ You can create folders on the iWork website by dragging presentations on top of one another, then naming the resulting folder. The folder then

continues on next page

appears in a similar way to folders on iOS . Clicking the folder opens it and shows you its contents.

▸ To delete a document from iCloud, click to select it, then press Delete, Backspace, or click the Actions button and choose Delete *filetype* from the pop-up menu. As usual when you are destroying data, iCloud will ask you to confirm your choice **H**. Click Delete.

TIP Frankly, it seems pretty lame that you need to mess with the web interface in order to update your iWork documents on your Mac. It puts the onus on you to remember to upload files to your Mac from your iOS devices when you want to work with them. As it turns out, there is a workaround, though not one sanctioned by Apple. This workaround allows iWork documents on iCloud to automatically synchronize between iCloud and the Mac. For more information and details about the procedure, see Ted Landau's article, "Bugs & Fixes: True sync of iWork docs between Macs and iCloud" in *Macworld* magazine, at `www.macworld.com/article/163291/`.

G Clicking a folder opens it, showing you the files within.

H You always have a last chance before you delete data.

What About iWork.com?

Since January 2009, with the introduction of iWork '09, iWork.com has been in "public beta," meaning people can use it but that its features may change. The website provides a web interface for viewing, commenting, and downloading uploaded iWork documents. One thing you can't do with iWork.com is edit the documents online, as you can do with a service such as Google Docs. What iWork.com is good for is sharing your iWork documents with other people. The website can accept uploads of Keynote, Pages, and Numbers documents and you can choose to share them with people either publicly or privately. You can also choose to allow them to download the documents, either in their native iWork format, PDF, or equivalent Microsoft Office formats for presentations, word processing, or spreadsheet documents.

If you're wondering what the relationship is between iWork.com and iCloud's Documents in the Cloud, well, there isn't one. The two services are, for now, completely separate. So to sum up, you would want to use the iCloud service to share your documents with yourself among your different devices, and you would use iWork.com to share your documents with other people.

Using iCloud to Find People and Devices

Need to find your iOS devices? How about your friends or family members? Or maybe your Mac? iCloud can help you with that. iCloud has a rich suite of services that allow you to find your iOS devices or your Macs, and locate them on a map. Once you've found them, you can send an audio signal, a text alert, remotely lock and add a passcode to the device, and even remotely wipe the device in the event of theft or loss.

Finding your iOS device isn't just useful in case of nefarious action. You can use the audio signaling feature to track down your iPhone after it has slipped out of your pocket and in between the couch cushions.

To find devices, you can use the iCloud website, or you can use Apple's Find My iPhone app, which runs on any iOS device. Another Apple app, Find My Friends, allows you to permanently or temporarily locate your friends (as long as they are carrying an iOS device).

Configuring iCloud Locating on the Mac

With Mac OS X 10.7 Lion and later, applications and websites can get and use information based on the current location of your Mac. For example, a web browser like Safari may ask for your location while browsing a shopping website in order to find good deals near you, or to determine nearby movie showtimes. Actually, the website you're browsing is asking Safari for your geolocation and Safari is passing the request on to you. You have to give your permission before the application or website can use your location information, which is handled by a part of the OS called Location Services (see the "Understanding Location Services" sidebar).

Understanding Location Services

Location Services is a part of Mac OS X and iOS that allows applications such as iCloud, Find My Friends, Camera, and Maps to determine your approximate location. Location Services uses information from the GPS (Global Positioning System) chips in your iOS devices, cellular tower triangulation in iPhones and iPads with 3G, and a database Apple maintains of public and private Wi-Fi hotspots. Your devices send location information to Apple continuously, but Apple says it does so in an anonymous fashion, so there is no way to personally identify and track you.

To determine your location, your device first tries to use GPS (because it offers the greatest accuracy). If you're not within a clear line of sight to the GPS satellites, the device tries to determine your location by looking for nearby Wi-Fi hotspots (you don't have to be connected to the hotspot; as long as your device can see it and it's in Apple's database, that's enough). If you're not in range of Wi-Fi, and you have a device with an active cellular connection, Location Services will try to calculate your approximate location by triangulating the distance to nearby cell towers (naturally, the location of every cell tower is known by the cellular carriers, and is shared with Apple).

Location Services often does a pretty good job of finding your iOS device, especially your iPhone (as long as it is equipped with GPS). It's less accurate with Macs. For more about accuracy, see the "Let's Talk Accuracy" sidebar, later in this chapter.

A You'll need to enable Find My Mac in the iCloud pane of System Preferences.

The Find My Mac service in iCloud uses Location Services, which in turn determines the approximate location of your Mac based on nearby Wi-Fi networks. You have to turn on the Find My Mac feature before you can, well, find your Mac.

If your Mac doesn't have Wi-Fi capabilities (like my old Mac Pro) or has Wi-Fi turned off, but is still connected to the Internet via Ethernet, you won't be able to use the iCloud website or the Find My IPhone app to locate that Mac on a map, but you can still activate the other features, such as Remote Lock and Remote Wipe, discussed in the "Using Find My Mac" section, later in this chapter.

To activate Find My Mac:

1. From the Apple menu, choose System Preferences.

2. In the Internet & Wireless section, click iCloud.

3. In the iCloud Preference pane, click the checkbox next to Find My Mac **A**. While you're at it, click the checkbox next to Back to My Mac. We'll be using that later in this chapter.

4. Close the System Preferences window.

There are two other places in System Preferences where you can deal with Location Services, if you're using a Mac with Wi-Fi. On all Macs running Lion or later, choose System Preferences > Security & Privacy > Privacy **B**. If you want to turn off Location Services (it's enabled by default), deselect the Enable Location Services checkbox. You'll probably have to click the padlock icon at the bottom of the window and enter your admin password before you can make this change. The list in this preference pane shows the applications that have requested your location. The checkbox next to an application name in this list indicates whether or not you have granted that application permanent location-finding ability. If the checkbox is unselected, the application will ask you each time it wants to use your location (for privacy reasons, that's the setting I actually recommend).

If Location Services is enabled and Wi-Fi is turned on, your Mac can set its time zone automatically using the current location. Choose System Preferences > Date & Time > Time Zone **C**. Select the checkbox next to Set time zone automatically using current location. Location Services will work its magic, put a red pushpin near your current location, and set the time zone.

B Location Services are enabled by default, but you can control them in the Security & Privacy pane of System Preferences.

C Location Services can automatically set your Mac's time zone.

Don't Be Lulled into Complacency

If your iOS device or Mac really is stolen, you have a limited window of opportunity to use Find My iPhone's features. If you remotely set a passcode or wipe the device, those events will only occur if the device is online and findable. If the thief is smart enough to quickly turn off Find My Device or turn on Airplane Mode, there's nothing you can do.

As usual, one good way to deter a criminal is to slow things down. And the best way to do that (and give you time to determine whether or not the device has actually been stolen or just misplaced) is to set a passcode for the device *before* you lose it.

On iOS, tap Settings > General > Passcode Lock, then tap the Turn Passcode On button. It's also a good idea to set the Require Passcode time to a short interval, and on the prior screen to set Auto-Lock to a short amount of time (I use one minute for both values).

On Mac OS X, choose System Preferences > Security & Privacy > General, then check Require password *pick a time from the pop-up menu* after sleep or screen saver begins.

Finding and Working with Your Devices

You can use the iCloud website or the Find My iPhone app, running on an iOS device, to find an iPhone, iPad, iPod touch, or Mac (see the next section for specific information about finding a Mac). It's important to note that you can only find the devices that you have already set up for use with Find My iPhone. Set those devices up now, so you can find them later.

To use the finding features, your iOS device must be using iOS version 3.1.3 or later. So you're not limited only to iOS devices eligible for iCloud (and therefore capable of running iOS 5 or later); even the oldest iPhone or iPod touch will work, as long as it was updated to the latest iOS version it could handle.

In this section, we'll be using the iCloud website to find and work with your devices. The Find My iPhone app, running on an iOS device, works similarly to the website, with minor differences because it's running on a mobile device with differently sized screens.

If you lose track of your mobile device, you will first want to try to find it. If it turns out that you didn't simply misplace the device and it appears to have been stolen, you can try sending a sound and message to the device. Next, you can remotely lock the device and add a passcode, preventing someone else from using it. The passcode must be entered before the device can be used. If all else fails, you can remotely wipe the device, which erases all the information on it, preventing a thief from seeing or using your information.

To configure your iOS device for location:

1. Tap Settings > iCloud.

2. Scroll down the list, then turn on Find My iPhone or Find My iPad or Find My iPod Touch, depending on your device **A**.

3. Press the device's button to close the Settings app.

To find your device:

1. Using a web browser, sign in to your iCloud account at **http://www.icloud.com**.

2. If the iCloud website brings you to the last application you are working in, rather than the iCloud home screen, click the cloud button at the upper left corner of the window **B**.

   The website brings you back to the home screen.

3. Click the Find My iPhone icon **C**.

A On your iOS device, turn on Find My iPhone in Settings > iCloud.

B If necessary, click the cloud icon in one of the other iCloud website applications to bring you back to the iCloud homepage.

C On the iCloud homepage, click the icon for Find My iPhone.

4. The application launches, and for security purposes, asks you to enter your iCloud password. Do so, then click OK.

The website displays a list of the devices you have activated with iCloud, with the selected device appearing on a Google map .

5. In the My Devices list, click the device you wish to find.

6. (Optional) As with all Google maps, you can use the controls in the window to zoom in or out, and switch from a standard map view to a satellite view, or a hybrid view that overlays street and location names over the satellite view.

TIP In the My Devices list, a colored dot will appear next to each device. A green dot means the device was recently located. A gray dot means that Find My iPhone is trying to connect to the device or that it can't be located.

TIP You can manually update the location of all your devices by clicking the Refresh button at the upper right corner of the My Devices list.

D You can select any of the devices in the My Devices list to display its location.

Let's Talk Accuracy

When you find your device, you should not necessarily expect pinpoint accuracy. The best accuracy will come from iOS devices that contain GPS chips. In my testing, I found that the reported location of my iPhone 4 could sometimes be within a few feet of where the device really was. My first-generation iPad (Wi-Fi with 3G model) usually didn't provide as much location accuracy, but the reported location was typically within 20 feet of the actual location. Both devices gave better results outdoors, where their GPS chips had a clear view of the sky. But even then, refreshing the website often showed the devices in a different location, even though they had not actually moved at all.

When GPS is obstructed (or the device doesn't have GPS at all), and the device falls back to Wi-Fi hotspot location or cell tower triangulation, you will usually see a large circle around the reported location of the device, indicating that the device is somewhere in that area **E**. Sometimes, as in the figure, that radius is quite large, and wouldn't be very useful in tracking down that wayward MacBook.

Using Find My iPhone can provide excellent results, but that depends on the device, whether it is outdoors, and other factors. It's a good service to have, but it's not a panacea.

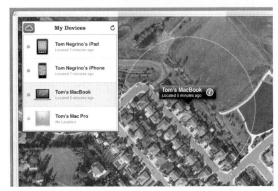

E The error radius when using Wi-Fi positioning can be pretty large; it's true that my MacBook is somewhere within that big green circle, but it really isn't very near the center.

F When you select a device, a popover shows its name, when it was located, and the blue Info icon.

G The Info popover allows you to work remotely with your device.

Info

Tom Negrino's iPhone
Located 1 minute ago

Play Sound or Send Message

Remote Lock   Remote Wipe

Cancel   **Send Message**   Send

Where are you, my dear phone?

Play Sound   ON

Sound will always play at full volume.

H To send a message or play a sound on your device, enter the message here, then click Send.

To signal your device:

1. On the map, your device will appear with its name, when it was last located, and a blue I (for Information) icon **F**.

2. Click the blue icon.

   The Info popover appears **G**.

3. Click the Play Sound or Send Message button.

   The Send Message popover appears **H**.

4. Choose one or both of the following:

   Enter a message that will be displayed on the device.

   Turn on Play Sound.

   continues on next page

5. Click Send.

Usually within a minute, the device will receive and display the message .

The iCloud website will send a confirmation email to the address associated with your Apple ID .

I The message appears as a notification on the lock screen of your iOS device.

Important Message
Where are you, my dear phone?

slide to unlock

From: **Find My iPhone** <noreply@me.com>
Subject: Your message to Tom Negrino's iPhone has been displayed
Date: November 4, 2011 11:07:14 PM PDT
To: Tom Negrino

Your message to Tom Negrino's iPhone has been displayed.

Tom Negrino's iPhone displayed the following message at 11:07 PM on November 4, 2011:

"Where are you, my dear phone?"

Use Find My iPhone on an iOS device or go to www.icloud.com/find on a Mac or PC to take additional actions.

 iCloud

iCloud Support | Terms of Service | Privacy Policy
Copyright © 2011 Apple Inc. 1 Infinite Loop, Cupertino, CA 95014. All Rights Reserved.

J The iCloud website also sends you an email confirmation whenever it interacts with one of your devices.

K To begin the Remote Lock process, enter a four digit passcode.

L After the device has been locked, the Info popover lets you know the process was successful.

To remotely lock and add a passcode to your iOS device:

1. On the iCloud website or with the Find My iPhone app, find your device.

2. Click the blue icon.

   The Info popover appears **G**.

3. Click the Remote Lock button.

   The Remote Lock popover appears **K**.

4. Enter a four-digit passcode.

   After you enter the passcode, the screen will automatically change to another screen asking you to reenter the passcode.

5. Reenter the passcode, then tap the Lock button.

   The iOS device will immediately lock, the Info popover on the iCloud website will reappear showing you the device has been locked **L**, and the iCloud website will send you a confirmation email. To use the device again, the passcode will need to be entered.

TIP If the iCloud website could not contact the device when you send the Remote Lock command, the Info popover will show a line that says Pending Actions and how long ago the lock was requested. At the bottom of the Info popover, you'll get a message saying that the device will be locked when it connects to the Internet.

To remotely wipe your iOS device:

1. On the iCloud website or with the Find My iPhone app, find your device.

2. Click the blue icon.

   The Info popover appears .

3. Click the Remote Wipe button.

   The Remote Wipe popover appears **M**.

4. Click the Wipe button.

   The data is wiped immediately, if the device is online. Otherwise, the device will be wiped when it reconnects to the Internet.

TIP Once you remotely wipe a device, it can no longer be found from the iCloud website or the Find My iPhone app. If you are truly convinced that the device has been stolen, wiping it can protect your important data (and then you'll be able to restore to a replacement device using either your iCloud backup or your iTunes backup). But if you think you have merely misplaced the device and you may be able to retrieve it, think twice about sending the Remote Wipe command.

M Are you sure you want to wipe your device? I sure wasn't; I chickened out and clicked Cancel.

Using Find My Mac

When you're using the iCloud website to work with a Mac, some things work in much the same way as with and iOS device, but with other things there are some differences. Finding and signaling your Mac work the same way as with a mobile device, so I refer you to the instructions earlier in this chapter to accomplish those tasks.

Things work a little differently if you want to Remote Lock or Remote Wipe a Mac from the iCloud website or from the Find My iPhone iOS app. First, it's important to note that Find My Mac is only available on Macs running iCloud, which is to say a Mac running Mac OS X 10.7.2 Lion or later.

All Macs running Lion have a feature called Lion Recovery, which is normally intended to let you repair your boot disk or reinstall Mac OS X Lion without the need for a physical install disc. The way that Lion Recovery works is that during the installation of Lion, the installer program creates an invisible read-only boot volume on your hard drive, called Recovery HD, which contains a variety of utilities that allow you to download and reinstall Mac OS X; use Disc Utility to repair or erase your hard drive; restore from a Time Machine backup; or browse with Safari to get online help.

The Remote Lock and Remote Wipe features in iCloud make use of this bootable Recovery HD. When you invoke Remote Lock from the iCloud website, you are asked to set a six digit passcode (a bit more secure then the four digit passcode you can set from the Find My iPhone iOS app). If your Mac is online, it immediately restarts and reboots from the Recovery HD volume, presenting a screen requiring the passcode.

If the Mac is off-line, the passcode lock happens the next time it's online.

As a last resort, you might want to use Remote Wipe. If your Mac is online, it immediately restarts from the Recovery HD volume, and begins erasing your boot disc, destroying all of its information. If the Mac is off-line, the erasure happens the next time it connects to the Internet.

TIP Interestingly, if you execute Remote Lock or Remote Wipe on your Mac, it's possible that you'll still be able to find it later with Find My Mac, because Lion also stores your iCloud credentials and the status of the Find My Mac feature on the Recovery HD.

To remotely lock your Mac:

1. On the iCloud website or with the Find My iPhone app, find your device.

2. Click the blue icon.

   The Info popover appears **A**.

3. Click the Remote Lock button.

   The Remote Lock popover appears.

4. Enter a six-digit passcode **B**.

   After you enter the passcode, the screen will automatically change to another screen asking you to reenter the passcode.

A To begin the Remote Lock process for your Mac, you'll start in its Info popover.

B Enter a six digit passcode for the Remote Lock.

C You can enter a message that will appear on the boot screen of your Mac after it has been locked.

D The iCloud website warns you that a locked Mac can't be wiped.

5. Reenter the passcode.

The screen will automatically change to another screen that allows you to enter a message that will be shown on your Mac's screen after it's been locked C. For example, you might want to enter your contact information so that someone who finds your Mac and is inclined to return it can easily do so.

6. (Optional) Enter a message.

7. Click the Lock button.

A confirmation dialog appears, asking if you really want to lock the Mac. It also warns you that a locked Mac can't be wiped D.

continues on next page

8. Click Lock Mac.

The Mac will immediately lock and reboot using the Recovery HD, the Info popover on the iCloud website will reappear showing you the device has been locked , and the iCloud website will send you a confirmation email. To use the device again, the passcode will need to be entered **F**.

Ⓔ After the deed has been done, the Info popover lets you know your Mac has been locked and rebooted into the lock screen.

Ⓕ This photo shows what my MacBook's screen looked like after it was locked.

Enter a six digit passcode for the Remote Wipe.

To remotely wipe your Mac:

1. On the iCloud website or with the Find My iPhone app, find your device.

2. Click the blue icon.

   The Info popover appears Ⓐ.

3. Click the Remote Wipe button.

   The Remote Wipe popover appears Ⓖ.

4. Enter and reenter a six digit passcode.

   The passcode will be needed to unlock the Mac even though the boot disc has been erased. The popover will automatically change to another screen that allows you to enter a message that will be shown on your Mac's screen after it's been locked and wiped. This might allow you to recover the hardware, even though you'll have to restore your data from a backup.

5. (Optional) Enter a message.

6. Click the Wipe button.

   A confirmation dialog appears, asking if you really want to wipe the Mac.

7. Click Wipe Mac.

   The Mac will immediately lock, reboot using the Recovery HD, and begin erasing the regular boot drive.

Using Find My Friends

At the same time Apple released iCloud and iOS 5, they also released a free new iOS app called Find My Friends. With this app, you can locate the iOS devices (presumably being carried by your contacts), as long as they've given you permission to locate them.

You can use Find My Friends in two ways. You can set up a list of contacts that you can locate all the time (for example, your close family members) and you can also set up temporary events to which you can invite people and that automatically expires at a set time. You might want to set up and use temporary events when you and a group of colleagues are attending a conference, or when extended family members are at a vacation spot, or when you and some friends are attending a concert or sporting event.

For privacy purposes, Find My Friends allows anyone who has authorized you to find their location to revoke that authorization at any time, and it also allows you to hide your location from all followers whenever you want.

Find My Friends requires iOS 5 or later, and all the participants must have downloaded the app to their mobile device. You can only use the Find My Friends features from the app; you can't use the iCloud website for this purpose.

To set up Find My Friends for the first time, download it from the App Store, then tap Find Friends on your iOS device **Ⓐ**. Enter your Apple ID (which is the same as your iCloud account name) and password. Tap Sign In, then confirm the app is allowed to use your location.

Ⓐ Tap the Find Friends app to get started.

B Sadly, you don't have any friends yet. Better click that Invite Friends button.

C You need to enter your friend's Apple ID in the screen, and optionally send them a personalized invitation message.

To add contacts permanently:

1. On the All tab of the Find My Friends app, it will initially show that you have yet to add any contacts **B**. Tap Invite Friends, or tap the Add button (+).

   The Add Friends screen appears **C**.

2. Type a friend's Apple ID, or tap the Add Contact button (+) to bring up your Contacts list. If you want, you can send a request to multiple people at the same time. You can also enter a personalized message.

   One drawback to the Find My Friends app is that it doesn't tell you which of your friends are also using the app, and, if they have multiple email addresses, which one of those is their Apple ID.

3. Tap Send.

   The app will show you a message explaining that after your friend has approved your request, he or she will appear in your friends list.

> **TIP** Just because you've sent someone a request and they approved it, it doesn't mean that they can also see your location. For that, they'll need to send you a location request as well.

To accept location requests:

1. Usually, a location request will appear as an iOS notification on the home screen. Tap the notification to launch the Find My Friends app.

2. Tap the Requests button at the bottom of the screen **A**.

3. Click Accept.

4. (Optional) If you're not already following the person who requested your location, and you want to add them to your friends list, tap the Ask To Follow button, which sends a request back to the person.

To locate friends:

1. Tap the All button at the bottom of the screen **D**, which shows a list of each friend and their general location. Then tap All Friends to display a map showing all of the friends in your list. On the map, your location will show a blue dot, and everyone else's map pins will be purple.

   or

   Tap a friend in the list to see details of their location and their contact information **E**.

D The All tab shows the friends you've permanently added, and their approximate distance from you.

E Tapping an individual friend in the list shows you their detailed location and contact information.

F You can get a map of your friend's location (shown here on Find My Friends on an iPad), and as usual that map can be a standard street view, a satellite view, or a hybrid of the two.

G To begin setting up a temporary event, you'll need to invite one or more friends.

2. To see your friend's location on a map, tap the address with the map thumbnail shown under Current Location, and the display will switch to the map view **F**.

3. (Optional) To contact your friend, do one or more of the following:

Tap the Send Message button to send a text message (you'll be prompted for which phone number or address to use; choosing your friend's iCloud address will send an iMessage, and choosing their mobile phone number will send a regular SMS).

or

Tap the FaceTime button to initiate a video conference (if the recipient has a capable FaceTime device).

or

Tap an email address to open the Mail app and compose an email.

Setting Up Temporary Events

If you only want to share your location with other people for a limited period of time, setting up a temporary event is just what you want. Find My Friends allows you to invite friends with a specified ending date and time, after which the location sharing automatically ends.

To set up a temporary event:

1. In Find My Friends, tap the Temporary button, then tap the Invite Friends button **G**.

2. Add the people you want to invite, give the event a name, and then tap the Ends field to choose a date and time the event will end.

continues on next page

3. Tap Send, and Find My Friends sends your invitation. If one of your recipients isn't already using Find My Friends, they'll get an email with the invitation (with instructions on how to download the app); recipients already using Find My Friends will receive an iOS notification, which they can accept or decline in the app .

H Everyone who gets an invitation to the temporary event has the chance to accept or decline it.

During the event, tapping the event's name shows you its participants and their approximate distance from you.

4. During the event, you can tap the Temporary button in the app to show a list of the event's participants . You can tap Send iMessage to send everyone a text message, or tap View Map to display a map with all the participants locations marked.

TIP Unlike permanent location sharing, when someone joins an event, they can automatically see everyone else who is part of the event, without each person having to exchange location authorization with every other person.

TIP If you are part of an event and wish to leave it, just tap the event name in the Temporary tab, then tap Leave Event.

TIP If you created the event, you can change the event name and ending time, remove or add participants, or delete the event.

Using Back to My Mac

Back to My Mac is one of the features that migrated to iCloud from MobileMe. It allows you to connect to one of your Macs from another Mac over the Internet. Once you are connected using Back to My Mac, it's just like being connected on a local network. You can mount volumes on the remote Mac for file sharing, or you can initiate a Screen Sharing session to control the remote Mac directly.

Imagine that you're on a business trip, and you're working in your hotel room on your Mac laptop when you realize that you left a vital file on your iMac at home. Naturally, you're not connected to your home network. But as long as you have turned on Back to My Mac before you left on your trip, you will usually be able to reach it from your room's Internet connection. You'll be able to mount the home Mac's hard disk as if it were just another network volume, and copy files back and forth between your local hard disk and your hard disk at home.

In the last paragraph, I said you could usually connect, because sometimes, due to poor or outdated network configuration in the location where you're staying, Back to My Mac just can't make the connection. That kind of failure to connect has become increasingly rare (Back to My Mac was originally introduced in 2007), but it still occasionally occurs.

In this section, we'll first show you how to configure your Mac so it can be accessed remotely, then show you how to use file sharing with your remote Mac, and finally show you how to start up a Screen Sharing session with the remote Mac.

TIP Besides connecting one Mac to another over the Internet, you can also use Back to My Mac to connect to a Time Capsule or AirPort Disk.

A The first thing you need to do is make sure that Back to My Mac is checked in the iCloud preference pane.

B You need to make sure that Screen Sharing and File Sharing are enabled on the Mac you'll be accessing before you leave home.

To set up your Mac so it can be remotely accessed:

1. On the Mac you will want to access remotely, open System Preferences > iCloud, then make sure that the checkbox next to Back to My Mac is selected **A**.

2. In the Sharing pane of System Preferences, select the checkboxes for Screen Sharing and File Sharing **B**.

   With both these types of sharing, you'll ensure better security if you click the radio button for Only these users in the Allow access for section, click the Plus button, and add your own username.

3. You will also need to enable Back to My Mac in the iCloud pane of System Preferences on the Mac that you are taking with you on the road.

TIP You must be signed in to iCloud with the same Apple ID on both computers for Back to My Mac to work.

To use file sharing on your remote Mac:

1. Open a window in the Finder. In the window's sidebar, the Shared section will show your remote computer, using its Computer Name that is set in its Sharing preference pane.

2. Click the remote computer in the Finder window sidebar. After a moment, the volumes that you have allowed to be shared will appear in the Finder window **C**.

3. By default, you will be connected as a Guest, which will prevent you from accessing files in your home folder. Click the Connect As button in the Finder window, then enter your username and password (to authenticate as a registered user), or click the Using an Apple ID button, which uses your iCloud credentials **D**.

4. You can now work with the remote files as if they were on any other file server.

C When you click the remote Mac in the sidebar of a Finder window, its available volumes appear.

D You can sign in for File Sharing as either a registered user, or you can use your Apple ID.

The Technical Stuff

In order for you to use Back to My Mac, your router for the network attached to the Mac you are trying to reach must support either UPNP (Universal Plug-And-Play) or NAT-PMP (NAT Port Mapping Protocol), and one of those services must be enabled. Virtually all modern routers support both or at least one of these protocols, and they are turned on by default, so you shouldn't need to adjust your router configuration.

Back to My Mac uses a combination of Bonjour (a protocol that allows services on a computer or device to advertise themselves on a network so other equipment can discover them), Wide Area Bonjour (which extends Bonjour to work over the Internet), and IPsec (a security protocol that creates a encrypted "tunnel" between the two computers).

Enter your name and password to share the screen of "Tom's Mac Pro".

Connect: ⦿ As a registered user
○ Using an Apple ID

Name: tom

Password: ••••••••

☐ Remember this password in my keychain

Cancel   Connect

ⓔ You can sign in for Screen Sharing as either a registered user, or you can use your Apple ID.

To share the screen of your remote Mac:

1. Open a window in the Finder. In the window's sidebar, the Shared section will show your remote computer.

2. Click the remote computer in the Finder window sidebar.

3. By default, you will be connected as a Guest. Click the Share Screen button in the Finder window, then enter your username and password (to authenticate as a registered user), or click the Using an Apple ID button, which uses your iCloud credentials **ⓔ**.

4. Screen Sharing will start, and a window displaying the screen of your remote Mac will appear **ⓕ**. You can click inside and work on objects in this window with your mouse and keyboard as if you were sitting in front of the remote Mac.

ⓕ Once Screen Sharing is started, you can see and work with the screen of the remote Mac.

Index

M

.Mac accounts, 9

Mac computers. *See also* lost or stolen devices
- adding to iTunes Match, 110, 111–112
- alternative calendar programs for, 64
- automatic iTunes downloading on, 105
- bookmark syncing on, 133
- bookmarklet installation on, 136
- configuring iCloud for, 12–13
- editing calendars on, 62, 75
- enabling remote connections to, 170–173
- Find My Mac service for, 148–151
- iCal calendar setup for, 58, 60
- iCloud Documents for, 142
- iCloud Mail setup from, 20–22
- iCloud requirements for, 6
- iWork version for iOS devices and, 141
- Lion Recovery for Macs, 159
- locking remotely, 160–162
- managing iCloud storage on, 126–127
- Photo Stream for, 93, 94
- receiving same Mail on iOS devices and, 20
- Recovery HD for, 159, 160, 162
- screen sharing for, 173
- streaming music from iCloud to, 113
- syncing contacts for, 47
- unable to wipe locked, 161
- using notes on, 28

Mac OS X Lion
- Lion Recovery for Macs, 159
- OS X requirements for iTunes Match, 110
- required for iCloud, 6
- uses for Apple ID on, 8

MacBook. *See* Mac computers

mac.com accounts, 9, 41

Mail (Mac)
- first time iCloud account setup in, 21
- illustrated, 21
- setting up iCloud account if you've used, 22
- working with notes in, 28

Mail preference settings (iCloud)
- Addresses, 41
- Composition, 42
- General, 39–40

- Rules, 43
- Vacation, 44

Manage Devices screen (iTunes app), 115

Manage Storage pane, 126

Manage Storage screen, 128

maps
- accuracy of Find My *Device*, 154
- finding friends on, 166–167
- locating missing devices on, 153
- opening from contact's addresses, 49

marking email, 36

merging browser bookmarks, 133

Messages app, 46

Microsoft Outlook, 84

MobileMe
- Back to My Mac feature of, 170
- calendars migrated to Calendar app, 59
- migrating to iCloud from, 15–18
- Photo Stream photo features vs., 96
- service and features discontinued, 5, 15, 20

Move to Folder icon, 32

movies, 108

moving
- contiguous email to folders, 35
- events on calendar, 75
- folders to another folder, 35

multiple Apple IDs, 9

Music app (iOS devices), 114

My Devices list, 153

N

naming calendars, 67

NAT-PMP (NAT Port Mapping Protocol), 172

Newsstand app, 106

Not On This *device* button, 107

Notes, 26–29
- about, 26
- appearing in Mail Inbox, 28
- configuring for iOS devices, 27
- creating, 27
- printing, 27
- Trash icon on, 27
- viewing on iCloud websites, 29
- working with in Mail, 28

O

operating systems. *See* iOS; Mac OS X Lion

P

passcodes
  remotely entering, 157
  required for Mac with Remote Lock, 159–160
  securing stolen devices using, 151
password for Apple ID, 9
phone numbers format, 56
Photo Stream
  about, 4, 93
  deleting photos from iCloud website, 102
  disabling, 99
  enabling, 95, 96, 99
  importing items to iPhoto or Aperture library, 99, 100, 102
  iPhoto preferences for, 99
  MobileMe photo features vs., 96
  setting up in iCloud, 94–96
  using Aperture with, 101
  using with Apple TV, 11
  working with photos in iPhoto, 93, 97–101
photos. *See also* Photo Stream
  automatically importing, 96, 99, 100, 102
  deleting, 96, 102
  downloading and uploading automatically, 96, 102
  importing to iPhoto or Aperture library, 99, 100, 102
  loading in HTML messages, 39
  MobileMe vs. Photo Stream, 96
  storage time on Photo Stream, 94
  transferring between devices with iCloud, 3
  uploading to all iOS devices, 98
POP mail protocol, 20
pop-up menus
  Actions, 36, 55
  Reply, Reply All, Forward icon, 34
Preferences (iCloud). *See also* System Preferences (Mac)
  Calendar, 82–83
  Contacts, 56
  Mail, 39–40, 41, 42, 43, 44

previewing mail messages, 39
printing
  contact cards, 55
  email messages, 38
  Notes, 27
  using AirPrint, 27
Printopia, 27
privacy
  Location Services and, 148
  preventing sharing of automatically uploaded photos, 98
  setting Mac preferences for, 150
private calendars, 77
public calendars, 79–81
Purchased in the iTunes sidebar, 108

Q

quotations in email replies, 42

R

re-downloading items on iOS, 107
read-later services, 132
Readability, 132
receiving location requests, 165–166
recovering stolen devices, 151
Recovery HD, 159, 160, 162
refreshing contact data, 55
Related People field, 51
reminders. *See also* Reminders app (iOS devices)
  about, 84
  adding list to iCloud website, 85
  editing or deleting, 87
  entering, 86–87
  features of, 58–59
  working with on iCloud website, 85–87
Reminders app (iOS devices), 88–92
  about, 88
  features of, 88
  reminders vs. alarms, 92
  setting reminders using, 89–91
Remote Lock
  enabling for Mac computers, 160–162
  locking and passcoding iOS devices, 157